Do You Know Who I Am?

Do You Know Who I Am?
Eric Lund

Eric Lund Publishing
2015

Copyright © TXul-856-398 2013 by Eric Lund

All rights reserved. This book or any portion thereof may not be reproduced or used in any manner whatsoever without the express written permission of the publisher except for the use of brief quotations in a book review or scholarly journal.

First Printing: 2015

ISBN <978-0-9964656-0-1>

Eric Lund Publishing
P. O. Box 345
Greenville, CA, 95947

Dedication

to my Mother

Always dedicated to, working for, the general welfare,
yet never neglectful of individuals caught or forgotten.
Always on the side of justice, peace and compassion,
    the humane choices.

CONTENTS

What Innocence Encounters	*	9 - 12
What Was Missed	*	13 - 14
walk to the lake	*	15 - 17
How It Can Happen	*	18 - 19
Perzeval	*	20 - 29
Huntington Gardens	*	31 - 34
Craftsman	*	36 - 40
The Resource of an Enemy	*	41 - 59
The Girl I Should Have Married	*	60 - 71
the limit	*	72
Translation	*	74 - 77
Reconceiving	*	79 - 81
Fate	*	83 - 176
Unpatriotic	*	178 - 194
A House Made of Glass	*	196 - 200
Aesthetic Lenses	*	202 - 231
sudden seasons	*	233 - 235
My Dad	*	236 - 267

Acknowledgements

I'd like to thank members of our writer's group for their feedback and encouragement

> Jan Cox
> Chuck Hanners
> Nancy Lund
> Marge Penley
> Linda Rean

The poem "What Innocence Encounters" was first printed in Kotasi Reviews, edited by Margaret Elysia Garcia.

What Innocence Encounters

Because the hill slopes so precipitously
a boardwalk had been built alongside the mobile home
running its entire length.

already dressed by their mother for outside
    after asking permission
a boy and his little brother
step out onto this deck.

The toddler has just learned to walk
    still can't talk
Joy, excitement,
    flicked with some apprehension.
Unsure, as if trying out stilts,
    great when they work
each jogging step a thrill.
checking down: behold the feet.
looking up: the whole beckoning hillside

Mature trees - mainly pine,
properties unfenced, boundaries unspecified.
poor rural Whites' disregard for appearance
pre-empted by each day's emerging urgencies.
  various once useful objects lie
  where last tossed.
old tires, chains, a broken sawbuck, rusted tools.
        abandoned
    nestled in place
        now belong there
the rust blends perfectly
with the old orange brown of the dried heaped leaves
and, where exposed, the ruffled clayish soil.

He prods his legs: go, try; with a hedging tentiveness.
Sometimes his legs marionette too-straight
then this tendency to curb possible mistakes

causes a foot to set down clumsily.
After all limbs have some weight,
and there is a lagging in compliance,
accentuated because he's having it both ways
    playing it safe
        while exploring the limits.

Clopping in one direction
coming to a swaying halt   bringing the two feet together
again looking down
wobbly turn
hurried foray back   another swaying stop.
again and again.
He's so happy.

The older boy, himself too young for school,
obviously loves his little brother
Though resentment and jealousy must mix in
  the latecomer's siphoning of attention
Pounces on him with a yell
  at the same time with steadying hands
he clutches his chest and back
  to prevent a recoiling fall.
The changes in expression on the small child's porcelain face
  - jumping at first with his heart –
body tightened in a fright reflex,
softening quickly to relief – the realization that it's play
delight at the switch,
to gurgling sweet laughter.
His brother bends down, right into his face
  so they can share the laugh.
It has about it the solicitous play we indulge a baby
taking on their entertainment wholly,
a performance dedicated-directed to one.

For awhile they occupy themselves independently.
Then suddenly, without warning,
the boy bumps the little fellow off the landing.

it was a thought   engaged curiosity   imagined
      then an urge
Inhibition   natural and taught
insufficient to resist/block the impulse
He just does it

The child, vulnerable on his halting colt legs,
taken by surprise - a blow he never sees coming -
thrown in the air like a loose-limbed rag doll
unable to control his body, or brace for the landing,
hits his head.
From the deck's edge his brother stares down at him.

strangely no sound for a long interval
the toddler is too stunned
needing a moment to gather himself
cope with the immediate throbbing pain
while figuring out what happened -
    his situation.
rather on its own natural release a cry escapes
  at first a sobbing whimper,
  hampered by his posture
    flopped over on himself.
the crying finds a cycle
working with breathing
and as he listens to the moan
  its forlorn tone
it confirms his pitiable state
  - the pain -
and the injustice.
prompting him to break anew
into a louder
even more mournful wail.

The older boy to cover the cry
and his own foul act
now yells out, "Mom! Johnny fell down."
She will assume it's that simple.

she has a lot to do
the little tyke, trapped in his tube of inarticulateness
   has no appeal
wrapped off in her inured sympathy that misses,
   they cross the scene - the truth not addressed.

With such transgressions the older brother will explore
   on his own
the possibilities of deception.
That fascinating invisible hemisphere
   with cross-whirling convolutions
      premeditated violations
      manufactured lies.
If you act deftly, knowing your target,
  so no alerts get tripped,
and are able afterwards to cover it with a convincing act,
You can penetrate forbidden places
  free there to work your will
  for good or ill.

The little fellow is prepped to beware
that in this new world
treachery can hide anywhere -
   any place, any creature.
behind the wonderful exteriors
with their surface Beauty
   unknown unseen motives
      circulate
   the predacious may lurk
   attack without warning
     with an intent to harm
        even to kill.

What Was Missed

How quickly the qualities
of a place
slip from awareness,
like a scent in a room
    when we decide to stay.

this loss aids us
as we work at ginning up our grievance
    at the unfairness of our fate
to be marooned in a drab gray nowhere
    stuck   dumb bad luck
    seemingly forgotten by Providence
    the absurd obligated chore(s),
the wasting of unstoppable Time
    which paradoxically - maddeningly
        won't move

If years later passing by
on a 'why not?' whim chose to enter
You are immediately overwhelmed
    too strong
    too familiar
Surprised by the palpable emotion
the air's drenching richness.
Frequent tasks touched to remembrance
    - with some pride.
  The unusual, that did occur;
  the odd characters, quirky tendencies,
  small activities and interactions
  that link to further memories.
everything now recalled fondly
Yes nostalgia plays a part in this,
an episode of your life (one you fled)
  preserved as a circumscribed whole,
it's natural to sentimentalize the past.
But there is more to this,

    the interval has allowed you
to reencounter the place fresh
to perceive the elements
    sensual and dramatic
that were always there,
    that had sustained you
long after you took them for granted
    (long after they became transparent).

walk to the lake

If every spring is spring
each is somewhat different.
This year, despite a couple of very warm interludes
the persisting cold seems to have delayed everything.
The oaks are still waiting   to leaf out
Where are the purple shooting stars,
   the white mountain iris, the lavender lupine?

When dogwoods open
not only are the stiff petals still cupped
     from the bud's ball clutch
          they're greenish.
if you don't know what they are - what to look for,
you won't see them,
   even though they're everywhere.
One year hiking with my nephew
- and I hadn't mentioned anything -
he asked why there was such a strong dog odor?
So I believe that is the origin of the name,
no matter what the nature guidebooks say.

Nearing the lake the road levels off.
There's quite a surprise this year
Two osprey have picked a ponderosa pine
that leans over the side, to build their nest atop.
These seem private birds,
why would they pick a tree right on the road?
Its so close to the road
the trunk is scarred, gash gouged-chewed,
by snowplows in winter hitting it.
The appeal must have been the top of the tree
which is flattened
perfect for lodging a large nest.
It will be a treat for me
to look for little osprey, see how they fare.

At the lake if you come upon a group of waterfowl
when you're noticed - all the ducks take off in fright,
flying hard and low to the far side of the lake.
The coots stay as they were, unconcerned.
They've learned that hunters aren't after them.
Today only a pair of tiny ducks
far enough out not to be frightened.
These dive underwater, and stay gone for so long,
you wonder. Just like with the grebes.

With the ice gone the fish have reappeared
  (where do they stay all winter?)
 blue gills in the shallows
 heads towards the land for some reason
   if its for insects its too early, there aren't any.
   they stay in place with slight sideways wiggles
    horizontal waves that pass through the body
       escaping at the tail.

On the range beyond there is still snow
and I wonder how it has survived.
Because they are so distant
I'm tricked into thinking the Sun hangs between us.
I don't realize the slopes I'm looking at
are really the back sides, away from the Sun.

On the way down
off on an old abandoned dirt road
a chickadee with thatch in its beak lands near me.
Little chickadees are so quick they don't fear man
They can work a tree downward,
    pecking and hopping,
     as easily as up.
The chickadee flies to the side of a stump,
looks at me, hesitates,
then disappears into a long hole.
I can't believe it's making a nest there,

so dangerously close to the ground.
Yet as bad as the idea seems
when it pops its head out to check on me
I quickly retreat
      to leave it in peace.

[This derives from memorable remarks made at a demonstration many years ago, during the Reagan years, at a protest of our government's collusion with the death squads in Central America. The speaker was one in a long line and all I recall from his hasty introduction was that he was a survivor of Auschwitz. There was no clever rhetorical structure to the speech that grabbed and kept your attention. It was what he said. Insights he wanted to share that he had learned from a unique experience.]

How It Can Happen

at morning all the buildings
convened back to where they'd been.
only the human carried fatigue over.

Spring didn't fail to come
Nature seemed wholly unaffected
trees leafed out
you could hear a troop of chirping birds
   swoop-scurrying pursuit through branches
the continuity could hypnotize
to wake from it you had to remind yourself
   of your condemned state.
The appearance in the camp
order   functioning   obedience
   modern impersonal mechanization
lent a veneer of rationality.
However all of it was machinery
   moved by dedicated hatred
   the spree intoxication of the demonic
   scapegoating   vengeance   insanity
Their diabolical sign "work makes free"
had long stopped conning anyone.
The guards, once young men
who had viewed themselves as patriots,
transformed into unfeeling devils in uniform
   herding humans to slaughter

         their job
murdering any worker-prisoner with impunity
    for the smallest trespass
what did it matter really?
    we were all slated to die.

The great secret of evil
    packed in with free will and being ourselves
    (whether you believe in God or Nature)
is that: determine to do something
no one comes from outside to interfere.

PERZEVAL

Q: It seems a long time since any news of 'exploits'.
Maybe you could untangle some of the stories we hear,
in what is now referred to as 'the Grail Mysteries'.
   Like a curse being placed on you?
   Were you really banished from the Round Table?
And please tell us what you're doing currently.

A: In the long slow sweeping tide of time
a whole generation came, grew up,
had children of their own.
While I have returned
   estranged
little better than a beggar.

         There is only one true son of the Fisher King.
         Those who know Know it is me.

However you want to term the quest
for the holy Grail
   the ultimate saga   search
      or trial
I committed myself with absolute dedication
and regarded nothing else.
There was no enemy that could deter me,
no obstacle that could stop me.
Every danger charged,
every challenge met and vanquished.
In my view rottenness reigned,
the nobility was thoroughly corrupt,
the rulers and their henchmen I slew
- or 'peacefully' overthrew –
one villain after another,
all deserving their fate.
If I ever sound contrite don't believe it,
their star was the Devil.

It's true that it wasn't long before I was alone –
make of that what you will.
Yet no matter how great the foe,
or how many their number,
with righteousness - the Lord's rod of iron -
I pounded all defiance into powder.

Though now a cause for shame
at the time I believed I possessed humility,
saw my power as a gift from the Lord,
was grateful for this blessing,
yielding credit back to Him:
  'It is by God's favor that I overpower.
  No man could have accomplished this.
  If it is His will that I raze the earth,
    I will comply.'
(I presumed that *was* the plan.)

A man can pass honors for a spell.
In the wake of the events
some days, weeks.
But the longer time stretches
the harder to resist
taking some portion for yourself.
Natural pride
- which no fair person can begrudge -
reconstructs itself into an edifice of vanity,
  'Is it not obvious that in courage, strength, and purity,
  I have surpassed all others?
  Surely the achievements themselves prove this.
  No knight – no mortal – has ever equaled these deeds.
  What other rival could claim the title INVINCIBLE?
  God doesn't make mistakes,
  and it was no mistake that He picked me.
  The fact that diviners discerned my coming
  before I was born
  confirms my Providential election.'

However I acted outwardly, whatever I said,
these were the thoughts boiling in my head.
Nor can I conceive that anyone in my position
could have had any other thoughts.
Though my mouth continued to cede
all credit to God
for giving me all these virtues
I was busy using the appearance of modesty
to burnish my perfect hero's luster even more.

I went on
with rare steed and sacred sword
cutting the enemies of the Lord to pieces,
until the awful day of realization & revelation

God has no enemies.

A chill went through me.
Instantly I knew it was true.
When I turned to look back
it was as if my eyes had never seen before.
Instead of a testament to heroic conquest
I beheld a trail of horrific carnage
only a fantastic beast could have wrought.
What sort of demonic deception had taken place?

That day, when I cast my sword away
(though I still believed it a blest instrument)
and, in penance, awaited death,
was the first day I truly incarnated courage.

But death did not come.

I became a pilgrim.
Deciding I should proceed as a penitent on foot,
I gave my horse to the first honest peasant I met.
I walked the earth,
seeking now absolution and salvation.

I can't explain
   given this devastating reversal
why I never lost my conviction
   that I alone was destined to find the Grail.

I wandered many years
   the geographies of the world,
encountering all the cultures, languages, people.
Every step I took in the world - going further,
   matched in my soul - going deeper.
     "The kingdom of God is within you"
       the truth slowly revealed itself.
   I wasn't searching for an object,
     a holy relic with sanctified power.
   The search was for a particular understanding.

In the end I found it

     All of Creation is sacred

This was the real Grail.
The truth hidden
while not being hidden.
And I, at last, possessed it.

I could now turn towards home.
I will not rouse you with a story
of what I should have thought;
transfigured meditations and insights,
lessons interwoven with the highest ideals.
Such tales can be great prompters for the young,
I don't in any way disparage their value.
But I will share with you the homely truth,
   hoping it can serve an alerting purpose,
most of the time I didn't have elevated thoughts.

   Q: Though you'd broken through?

A: I couldn't – or didn't – hold onto it.
It was a rapid fall from grace,
a collapse into an ugly self-pity.
Instead of meditating on the revelation,
or on what I had learned as a pilgrim,
I indulged the memories of triumph,
I kept going back to my days as a knight.
That's what I dwelt on. My illusional glory.
Like one who has been robbed, I felt a great loss,
    as if I had been tricked and wronged.
Its not that I wanted to be hailed or celebrated,
but I couldn't accept that all my heroic deeds,
the extraordinary vanquishings I took such pride in,
could be swept away, add up to naught.
That the final evaluation of those efforts should be
    that the bad exactly balanced out the good.
I felt this was a nullification of my whole life.

I should have bowed to the wisdom of the Grail,
accepted the truth and changed forever what I valued,
    grasping that it had to go the way it did.
But whatever elasticity I had started with had dried.
I couldn't stretch myself to accept this annulment.

Disillusion.

At the onset I had been promised that with success
the kingdom would be mine for the asking.
I can attest this promise has been kept.
Though I brought back no tangible proofs,
those entrusted with the regency believe me,
and are prepared to invest.

There is a riddling wrinkle, catch or twist,
that prophecies often bring.
I'm not sure I want the kingdom.
I'm not sure the people want me.

They seem to have spoiled in the interval.
There is no trust, benevolence, or loyalty in them.
At least not visible to me.
I always loved humanity
but in the abstract - from a great distance.
What I see is decay
a state that accords with their petty, deformed souls.
Their rumors about me are low and inane:
  'He's deceitful. He never found the Grail. His story is a lie
    to cover that up.'
  'He's deceitful. He inherited the Grail. And everything else.
    But he's keeping it all for himself.'
  'He defected. That's how he survived. By going over to the
    other side.'
  'He succumbed to depravity. For that he was cursed, banned
    from the Round Table, judged unworthy of the Grail.'
They're so stupid they can believe
    all this contradictory rubbish in turn.
The sort of malice that would have wounded my younger self,
now it neither touches or surprises me,
simply confirms and deepens my disenchantment.
Putting aside the idiotic rumors and gossip
I don't resent or even reject the underlying presumption -
    that Perzeval failed.
More in feeling than thought I'm inclined to believe that's true.

Q: You acknowledge that?

A: I give you my earnest vow that when I started
I had the basis of something better.
Yet everything Merlin foretold has come to pass:
    "There is no doubt Perzeval
        that you are the one of God.
    Yea all will fear you.
        Not just the bad. The good as well.
    And they will be right to fear you.
    No one can survive your 'purification'.

You find everyone lacking.
    The nobility and their appendages:
        with souls of corruption;
    commoners as gross corporality.
What distinguishes you Perzeval
is that you alone never asked
    'What do I want?'
Nor did you act from loyalty to your own
    (despising as you do everyone).
Only you acted solely for the good.
There is great charity in your acts.
    None in you.
When you look at the people you only see
the result: the stuntedness and ignorance;
    not the deprivations that caused it.
Contempt is not a manner of distinction,
    it is a grave fault.
    You will reap endless triumphs,
    but they will turn into air.
There is narrowness in your accusations,
the way you place them on people,
judging responsibility,
    while refusing to look at beginnings."

While Merlin was the greatest magi of all
his prophecies weren't magical.
A terrible curse had been allowed -
recompense for his extraordinary powers.
He had to live his life backwards.
Every waking was the day before.
That's why he struggled not to fall asleep.
The fatalist knew the future in great detail
because - for him - it was the past.
All he said about me is now engraved.
The fact that I could do what I did,
then dwell on my snatched glory
not on the monstrous slaughters,
  makes suspect my declared repentance.

All things seem to share this trait,
an innate disposition to disappoint,
    to curl at their end.

Q: Well we know when a monk takes holy orders
he forsakes worldly goods and comforts;
vows to accept poverty, chastity, and obedience -

A: No no no, it wasn't some noble renunciation.
You're getting it all wrong. Nothing like that.
Obedient? I'm not sure I've ever been obedient.
And I don't presume people will be better off
    governed by others
- in fact I presume the opposite.
Look I searched for the Answer and I found it,
    yet I look at my life and its empty.
    Love and children fill a life.
As one who always stepped forward to the call
only later to find his actions a hollow shell,
    his achievements a guilty burden,
I have no appetite for further such duties.
The prospect of new expectations to fulfill
has no appeal. I cannot be bothered.

    God may judge me
    but where is the man who has the standing?

Q: I'm not confident people are going to understand
what you're saying. What it all adds up to.

A: Alright listen, the sages,
the only ones who know what I have done,
who see my journey as fulfilling some divine plan,
    all the circumstances,
    all the decisions – including the mistakes,
    labors, earned wisdom,
to them it falls and fits in some ordained order,

>   they are excited and pleased.
> I do respect them. I trust I honor their wisdom.
> I am glad, sincerely, that they are satisfied.
> And their advice, I am sure, is sound and pertinent.
>   I heeded all that once
>   never again.

Q: What do they say about your future role?

A: Since I'm the only one who learned the truth
       in exactly the right way,
I'm the only one who understands it
       in exactly the right way,
I'm the only one who can explain it
       in exactly the right way.
Which is: so everyone can understand,
       and no one can understand.
Doing the impossible - how everything's done.

Q: Excuse me, I'm not sure I'm following why
the 'no one can understand' part is desirable?

A: I think it just mirrors the way things are.
You get all the way to the end and you find out
there's a doubleness to everything.
Anyway that's what they say I must - and will - do.
But I repeat: I have no inclination to do anything.
Certainly not to challenge usurpers.
I will enjoy watching the competition, like a sport.
And just between us - I will root for the worst.
My contesting days are over.

Something I've noticed recently. A weakness.
Not of the warrior variety - loss of strength,
     or cowardice that weakens with doubt.
I could kill the best of the contenders
     with a tree branch.

No I'm speaking of that inner binding force
    everyone has, must have, to hold a purpose
and sustain their efforts. It's bled away.
Probably because I lost my will and dedication.

I remember when I was young how intrigued I was
when a man of experience and accomplishment
would reach some private limit, turn in disillusionment,
and decide to have nothing more to do with the world.
How fascinating and admirable their total wordless resolve.
Of course this rejection was also puzzling and threatening.
Funny fate if now, as it seems, I've become
    one of those strange disenchanted figures.

Q: But the whole exchange of the sword for the quill
was divinely designed so you'd write what you found
- I assume that 'all of creation is sacred'. Right?

A: Yes, but part of the truth is that
    it can only be understood
        by those who already know it.
I'm sure there's an enhancing value in reminding
those who know what they already know,
but it's hardly compelling is it?

As to worldly success
the only one I wanted to impress, my Father,
    is dead.
So what does it matter?

I know I should care
but I don't

our core knows

Huntington Gardens

Once somewhere to go

a place that is no more
though it's more popular than ever
an L.A. sight
   in fact its probably the throngs
   that wore its soul away
     (contempt for tourists
      except when they're us)

in my past
Huntington Gardens
had been an escape
  from LA heat and humdrum
not weekends – too crowded
weekdays the visitors were sparse,
   you could wander at your own pace
   leisurely tour
   what that day caught your fancy
as if you'd slipped surreptitiously
over onto the grounds of a rich neighbor,
   reconnoitering   roaming
    if not by invitation
     not prohibited either

It had been years
  where once it was free
  not any longer
The administrative staff had always been petty
but they had no jurisdiction over the gardens
   or library.
Now with the influx
  maintenance costs, a large gift shop,
   they apparently run the show.

signs everywhere warning no walking here
   I didn't care – I tramped through the brush
   I had to check
   how the dawn redwoods were doing   (fine)

It was certainly not the trees or flowers' fault,
They were all still in their old places,
   the early rose varieties back of the house,
   and down on the lower level
     the cactus garden, lily ponds,
       the grass fields and trees from Australia,
          but it felt disappointing
             smaller   slighter   sadder.

It might have been nothing more
   than the mood I happened to be in
or a reaction from spending years in a forest
   to the obviously planted and tended
     coming off as too tame
     as if their role, representing different species
        to all these visitors
     had turned them into flat icons
        that could no longer serve
        to launch the imagination into reverie
     as they once had
     when I was a trapped city dweller.

My favorite times to visit -
   LA can get so hot
   you can't think
   and when hot – smoggy,
had been when a storm came in
or the day after a rain
   a world cleaned
   everything shining
the change
maybe a cool breeze
even fewer people

the clouds as reprieve
even full overcast
   the day dark
emotions seemed stronger
     moisture
the light more dramatic
people more beautiful
everything more beautiful
not a trick either.
Plain has a truth
but beauty is real and equally valid.
the additional facets and force
   shading yields
   color richness
   features resolved with more depth
    existing, simply made visible
     and heavier
Maybe feelings are like sound
requiring, as a medium, substance
blocked by emptiness
   this doesn't occur to us
   because we think of air as empty
   (which of course it isn't)
So in a way we *touch* music

                        one such heart-full day there
                        under the partially covered patio
                        I stared as mist collected
                        on a thick glossy camellia leaf
                        into one clear drop
                        developing emotional significance
                        the leaf nodded slightly to the weight
                        then the drop rolled
                           a beaded trail
                        to the leaf edge
                        hung on for a very long time
                        not letting go

                finally did separate and drop
                the leaf bobbing
                    as it sprung in recoil

I remember another day getting caught
    when the rain shifted
deciding it would come down really hard again.
I didn't have to worry about getting too wet
and afterwards soiling my car's interior
as I drove my old beat-up station wagon
   which I hauled tools and chemicals in
     doing my pool route.
At one point I was running in a cloudburst
           with a joy
   that kept brimming out into laughter
     soaked and not caring
   somehow that made it more celebratory
    a brief unexpected childlike happiness
      free
       you feel like running
  (if you were all alone you might dance)
Knowing the layout so well
I headed for a little portico I knew of
that covered an always-locked side door.
only looking up at the last minute to see
   a family, all adults, aghast -
 They had taken shelter there before me
alarmed to see this drenched longhair
laughing like a madman
running straight at them.
I veered, apologizing as I did,
   running on further
though I did catch a rueful smile
on the face of the daughter.

People are never as bad as they seem

Craftsman

When I was fairly young but years after
I'd come to see myself as a writer
some lines came to me

> *Magic bus*
> *enchanted mind*
> *craftsman*
> *of the highest kind*

With the exception of early childhood
(and even that had the mystical experience)
throughout my life odd things,
like communiqués from the Spiritual - intuitions
and even events, would occasionally happen.
So I didn't react to this like a normal person,
I took the lines as aimed at me,
    and not as something I'd made up.
To show you what a pretentious young fool I was
    – how stuffed with nonsense -
instead of being flattered and pleased
with the 'enchanted mind' part, what I focused on
and reacted to, was my failure to make 'artist' grade.
"Craftsman"?
Most people probably couldn't tell you the difference
    between artisan and artist,
but in my mind then the distinction was everything.
An artist composed with the ideal and the essential
    - in the element of the spiritual.
The inspiration was of an elevated nature.
Lowly crafts people weren't creators or visionaries.
The good ones were in harmony, flowed with Nature,
    but they felt their way, manipulating the earthen.
We'd have to acknowledge they were 'in tune',
    but it wasn't a master artist's conscious creation,
it was more going with - allowing yourself to be ruled.

Why would Providence demote me like this?
    Not grant me my due as an artist?
If someone challenged me now: 'You're not a real artist'
I wouldn't have the warrant to retort 'Yes I am'
    (believe it or not this has never come up.)
I couldn't pretend 'craftsman' was a slip.
The Absolute doesn't admit mistakes.
Well the Absolute doesn't make mistakes.

Of course I couldn't talk to my skeptical father
    about anything supernatural.
Though he revered Beethoven, Rembrandt, Burns, et al,
I think he would have been pleased that his son
got grouped with workers and tradesmen. Real men.
While he admired the geniuses of art, and their works,
for life lived it was safer to stay clear
    of that type of ego,
    byproduct of a fanatic dedication
        which required inhabiting an isolated sphere,
    mental and physical separation from ordinary people,
        from 'real' life and the 'real' world.
Putting on airs, getting so full of yourself,
eccentricities that risked turning you into a phony.

            And as much as my younger self yearned
                for a higher appellation,
            if to qualify required me to spool out
            impressive evocations of abstruse ciphers
            in artificial formulations,
                far removed from anything observed
                (pretense, lack of any significance),
            then, with a sigh,
            I would have had to resign myself
                to the lower classification.
            With the possible exception of Rilke
                - and maybe Rimbaud? -
                the poetry I loved was plain and direct.
            The haiku poets, Wordsworth, Machado,

        Dickinson, Whitman,
     our contemporaries who are genuine.

Not dabblers with solipsistic puzzles,
each poem containing its own strategy,
   dense, hip and obscure,
     art object
     empty as a balloon.
Some even resorting to breakage
   abandoned fragments
     of words
       perceptions
       sensations/experience
       philosophical ideas
   fake accounts of consciousness.
But broken pieces don't cohere.
My favorites used the common language,
   earnestly desired to be understood.
Difficulty wasn't added as spice.
If it arose it came from following
the contours and complexities in the world
   and in its truths.
Even when their subject was small,
   as part of life it got magnified.
Poetry wasn't cleverness or performance
   - playing a poet.
The intentionally obtuse
   has no substance that allows it to endure.
The first impression can trick us,
   its not the last.

Have I become an envious petty begrudger?
   'I merely turn straw into gold.
     Let's see your hoity-toity artists do that!
     And no, my name is **not** Rumpelstiltskin.'
       (What a small man I am.
       Maybe I am Rumpelstiltskin.
       I better watch out for hopping.)

Providence's tag did accord with how
I eventually came to see the process.
There is a period when the material is molten
    workable   formable
you can shape it, try different approaches.
Things you don't expect appear, get added
    together – flowing into the melt.
Welding on pieces from outside;
    cutting excess, grinding - buffing.
Hammer each sentence, each word.
    And it is *work*.
Eventually though a time comes
    (for me its usually measured in years)
when it sets.
Whatever your misgivings - its done.
Arrived at – it is what it is.
    and you must walk away, leave it.
Accept that that's its final form.

Older, I've not only loosened my hold
    on that aspiration to 'high art',
but also the scorn apprentices are schooled to apply
    against establishment gatekeepers
whose minds and tastes supposedly controlled by the past,
    predictably unfair and blind to living innovation,
and the imagined Philistine mob
ignorantly conflating worldly success with artistic value.
Now though, after I tell someone I'm a writer,
I feel an obligation to add hastily:
    "One who's never made a red cent from it."
No longer certain that this isn't relevant or indicative.

After a few decades I think I did
    finally resolve the bus riddle.
The origin of bus, omnibus,
indicates a collection of some variety.
Beyond a lumbering slow vehicle

it also connoted the sort of course a bus follows.
My inability to think or speak in straight lines,
everything circling, spiraling,
matches a bus route: predictable course
multiple stops   turns   circuit.
Possibly I wasn't just a passenger
   but the driver – driving others.
All these years later I have to bow
      to that Judgment
whatever it finally turns out to be.

       As I look back it seems Providence
           measured me to a T
       choosing *bus* and *craftsman* shrewdly.
       Knowing 'bus' would intrigue
         - a puzzle to be solved;
       while 'craftsman' would bug me,
       I'd keep working at it - to refute it.
       Together I wouldn't be able to put
       the assessment aside and forget it.
       And when I was mature enough
         I would understand
           and accept.

       Though I didn't catch on at the time
       God was telling me to think long term.
         That I was long term.
       Informing me in an appropriately
         spread out manner.

The Resource of an Enemy

"Those who will always promote war still need to justify it."
                                    -- A.J.P. Taylor

I. Awakened by Death

unknown dark enemies disclose their existence
in a surprise attack

                 They pick a pretty morning,
                 the city street walked as a riverbed
                 at the bottom of a glass canyon.
                 sunlight reflections aslant
                 glinting yellow and pink
                 air fresh from the nearby ocean.

                       Catastrophe!
                          pause
                  another plane oblivious
                   enters off course
                     as in a dream
                        turns
            smashes itself through the brother tower
                 'We're under attack!'

                     clever stealth
               to commandeer large jets
               and fly them into our skyscrapers.

We don't want to be Rome/Babylon
     (even though we are)
Making the world One
     Knowledge
     Commerce
     Culture
     Force

Spectacle
  visual - it can't be real
its happening like a demonstration
speed of the collision – jet fuel flung
bowling through, puncturing out the other side,
  effect created-while-we-watch
Yet it must be
as we wake - as our hearts pound to see
We have to affirm - tell ourselves it's really happening.
it connects to a visceral fear we have in skyscrapers
their unnatural extenuation pushing luck
  how at the mercy of things we'd be
  if for some reason they snapped.
We have to assume there are a lot of people cut off up there.
Then smaller horrors
human figures separating and falling off the sides
individuals like ourselves provided no way of escape
pushed by fate into casting their lives away
Flames coming at their skin
choosing to jump
  out into space - hope
dropping by the face of these huge unperturbed buildings
constructed squared-off mountains
with their grand inhuman scale.
The fragility of a small vulnerable body in this landscape
  the physical thrill of falling
  speed created wind
  knowing life ends at the closing ground.

In the back of our mind comes the thought
that we must have inadvertently trespassed
some foreign foe
dedicated now to our punishment.
They've unfurled this planned devastation
a declaration
of such hardened zeal and hatred
  it must have a back story

discarded dogs
subsisting somewhere in the furthermost precincts of the empire
   swarthy castes
   walking proudly in sandals and robes
   midst the blowing dust
     somewhere very remote
     where soccer is the only game
       because all you need is a ball.

                    Once important
                    (still important to themselves)
                    Spiritually rich
                    - their one endowment
                    Our dismissive contempt
                    was somehow threatening.

To us they seem dirty.
Who knows if they really are?
Maybe instead of killing them
we should give them a good scrubbing.
Is this an association with waste –
or the circumstantial dirt of the poor?

that we don't control what happens to us
Airline passengers tricked
ordinary people believing they were on their way
  to the stated destination.
A hijacking. Fear. Ghastly deception
      sudden death
   Were they not innocent?
Office workers
ordinary people who showed up to work
as on any other day
      sudden death
   Were they not innocent?
Firemen

one of the few heroes to survive childhood
the power they reached for
- unlike police or soldiers -
is wholly to do good.
Bravery tested
  combating the consuming element.
risking their lives to rescue people
  when possible - their homes.
Doomed by duty this day
to enter the high rise sepulchres
        sudden death
  Were they not innocent?

> *They hate us.*
> *for no reason they hate us.*

Collective guilt?
Can that ever be right?

> *We will kill them all.*
> *See if we do not do it.*

Of course we witness this
the strange intrusion into inert routine life
      by real life
on TV
awakened from our normal viewing trance
 (the flowing/blinking/folding continuance
 liquid forms inside our magic glass acquarium
 that little world all surface able to suggest depth
 while subliminally suggesting all is surface)
Helped by the adrenaline now in our system
we keep telling ourselves
  - as if we need the reminding -
  that this is real – and happening now –
  and need to compensate for the violation of viewing.
The change in the news anchors. They stop performing.
The reporters become themselves. Just people there.

The city authorities,
including the mean mayor,
facing the calamitous collapse -
take charge with skill, compassion and honesty.
People rising to the occasion.
There is more in us than it appears.

                Like a soldier unable to accept
                his buddy - killed in a flash blast
                   turned into a mess of meat
                we stumble towards denying disbelief,
                Yet we know all caught inside are gone.

The network switches to the West Bank
Palestinians celebrate with glee in the street
honking horns, throwing candy,
   whooping it up.
To them we are nothing but Israel's guarantor.

We aren't happy to see your civilians die.
We don't even like the Israelis anymore.
We're just stuck - historically - politically.
The Palestinians' prolonged degradation-beating
has made them stupid and shortsighted.
Like their support for Iraq's invasion of Kuwait.
the penalty for this brainless display
     will be measured in years.
They literally 'dance on their own grave'.

    On a rooftop with a view of the twin towers
    another group dances in celebration.
    A team of Israeli agents.
    They are happy - not for the act -
       but for its obvious consequences.
    Israeli Intelligence had discovered the plot
    and sent them to monitor the attack.
    They know the U.S. will be forced now
      into an even tighter embrace.

The enemy's secrecy and grim determination
meshes with predestined luck
(plus a flaw in the structural engineering),
the incredible heat from the fires unleashed
melts the steel supports on the levels hit.
The stories above – squares of concrete
push till the weakened skeleton breaks.
     a waterfall in
a great stacking collapse
no floor strong enough to stop it
each gets added on
becoming a force so great
that when it hits the ground
each tower splashes
   into a great cloud of powder.

We must accept natural catastrophes
        Acts of God
  Earthquakes, hurricanes, volcanoes, avalanches
  even accidents, epidemics and famines.
No matter how inconsolable to a loved one
in the broadest view
it's lodged with the necessary conditions
  that come with this world.
This violation of order is harder to take
  because manmade.
Some individuals far away conspired,
to them the people who would be harmed
were inconsequential phantoms.

They must hate us all.

                The dead infer
                  as they always have
                we have gotten
                so attached to this age
                that we shall never leave.

II. Consequences & Rationalizations

Yes our culture is commercial and shallow.
If so disposed you could draw a composite profile
reduced to this mean.
Where's the surprise?
It's the assay of man.
Survey the barbarians, they'll fare no better,
exchanging crude for superficial.

We won't argue for our popular culture,
We will dispute that it captures all we are.
We will dispute that we force it on others.
   don't buy the hamburger
   don't go to the movie
   don't listen to the music
What do we care if you spurn
    our inferior food
      or envy our superior lives?

                All our sins
                are the sins of humanity.
                This is what people are
                    when free

There is a desire by many (the devout)
and those who want to divorce
the Absolute from responsibility
   to say the tragedy isn't what God wanted
   its the work of men.
while it has its truth
   and is comforting
it also promotes a fiction
to mask the hardness of the world.
the Absolute includes everything
this
like everything else
is part of the whole, part of the plan.

People have a response
when snubbed by a different culture
     a new age
     a civilization metamorphosizing
        growing prospering
    indifferent to their holy book
to go into themselves
and there fashion a schema
that reestablishes the old law as still apposite.
They cast the new attitudes – and their agents
   as lost debauched/intoxicated damned.
The trouble really comes from being caught
   between two worlds.
But the story they tell themselves is the ancient one:
  Evil hates the good
    tries to seduce
    tries to force
  assaulting everything the good holds onto.
Then they ask, 'Are we not justified in striking back?'
    personal religious to act
   'Is this not self-defense?'

They took the trade towers as advertised
  That we'd doubled Babel.
    Want to prosper?
    We are the hub.
    Our commerce the model
    better learn English.
They chose landmark targets -
the towers, the pentagon, the capital.
The plan was to destroy the top of the towers,
  putting them out of commission.
When both buildings collapsed to dust
they took it as a sign of Divine approval,
when it was the opposite - done to provoke
  absolute doom down on them.

In the immediate appraisal
no doubt our hubris
our willful disdain of others
deserved - and received - a comeuppance.
However the real judgment fell on them.
We may be Rome
but if so, they are the Jews
rebelling against Rome.

                                            What grows lives
                                            What lives grows

As frequently happens with the immoral
the people the power elite (cynically) used
turned to bite us.

Leaders of the fight against the Russians
the glory of that victory
safe, wistful of the lost thrill -
    days full alive
  every moment your life at risk
Esteemed by their people as heroes,
they start to believe their own myth
    as noble figures
      fighting to preserve the religion
      making history as they acted.
Missing this they looked for a fitting foe
   so they can resume that role,
and who is bigger than us?

                                      What we know about men
                                    is that they shift their beliefs
                                      till they're allowed to do
                                    what they want to do.

        Why do we have to kill each other?

We are still a democracy
Our people
still believe in our principles.
when the time is right
   we can clean
      our minds
      our media
      our government
   of the impurities
   and blockages
the plutocrats and the greedy
   have left in our way
   like readymade rubble.

     When the people have had enough
     they will change the system's structures.

We assume those willing to sacrifice their lives
must be stalwarts of faith.
In fact the opposite is true.
A person of solid faith
  accepts the conditions of the world,
  is not threatened by what others believe,
  nor that they happen to be thriving.
It is those who are struggling,
  who are caught midway
who get perturbed by what they see,
  mix it with their internal conflicts.
It is to them that violence appeals.
    Let's get it over with
       resolve the uncertainty
          decide things.
Physical acts that will
convince themselves,
their family, friends, community,
that a soul weak and shallow,
was brave and holy.

hate
hatred   a black pool
   immersing the soul
those the hater fixates on
lose all human characteristics

to rely on hating is a personal weakness
to indulge in scapegoating
to be impressed by unrestrained violence.

We acknowledge our lapses,
greed and prejudice,
illegal and immoral acts.
But there was also a lot of hard work.

Unlike the Europeans,
who for centuries divided everything into
my advantage = your disadvantage;
now conveniently label all history as criminal
    and all humanity as corruptible;
or their backward prey,
the serfs and savages,
who simply fabricate fanciful fictions;
We don't excuse or whitewash the past.
We believe in learning and growing,
in our own capability and goodness,
    and in the worth of others.
We subscribe to truth as a helpful medicine.

Produce all our serious transgressions;
mindful that most turned on decisions of a few,
- the damned - who lied and played on us.
We are still prepared to stand for Judgment,
confident good will outweigh bad.
Unlike any nation in history since Rome
that has enjoyed dominion,
  we were sincere in believing
      everyone could prosper,

and we wanted them to prosper.
Truly we possessed goodwill towards all.

Who could have guessed
landing on the Moon was our apogee?

In the world's cold future
they will miss our lead
   robust Americans.
Only in absence recalling our virtues
   know-how with creativity
   upbeat attitude
   industry
   humor
   refreshing egalitarian informality
     and disdain for hierarchy
     not just in words – in our behavior.
Enthusiasm, openness, energy and benevolence;
all the characteristics of the constructive.

Not to say we shouldn't have lived closer to our ideals.

We should have been more interested in others.
We should have shared more of our wealth.
The moral obligation of the richest nation in the world
  to pull up the poorest.
But our economic creed was survival of the fittest;
and as a giant continent-country
   our own interests and problems
   claimed most of our attention.

          We grew too materialistic
            too selfish
          But that's surface stuff
            we can slough off

III. Resolution & Vengeance

Like a river life's continuity flowed on
the shock – the unacceptableness –
(the effect the attack had on that day)
   wore away
and as is often the pattern in malleable reality
got supplanted by its opposite.
At first breakage, now integral to that time.
with this came a feeling   an intuition
so subversive we had to suppress thinking it
   (as if you could quarantine your own thought,
      maneuvering to wall in a part)
that there was something wholly renewing
facing a real enemy again.
One that had no compunction to kill,
who fiercely disregarded all the rules.
Like a person hit with a threatening diagnosis
   our lives had become vital again.
Value imbued in all of it
the little things we did every day
All that was familiar became dearer
We were more alert, more appreciative.
Where once in airless routine boredom
we would have questioned
   the meaning of our life
Facing cancellation we feel its preciousness
as close as our heart's pulse.
Our cause
   which was fundamentally ourselves
appeared justified. Purely defensive.
After all we were attacked by alien fiends.
To be evil's foe restored us back to good.

      We didn't know. Now we see.
      No matter how hard the task,
      length, demands,
      including some of our young,

the hard stretch
when it becomes slow work;
the repugnant slaying of unknown strangers;
We thank Providence for the challenge
  in giving us a diabolical foe.
Our founders fought the brave Indians
lawless savages
unseen in the dark forest
inscrutable   unpredictable
erupting into massacres.
Our grandfathers the Germans & Japanese
acting like swarming evil automatons
apocalyptic plague of mechanical insects.
Now we have our own
scary religion-mad savages
- unreachable by reason – out to kill us.
They don't have a normal army or state
but its an age of catastrophic weapons
    even nuclear and biological.
No price could be placed on this.
We shall reveal our true mettle
in a fight none dare say isn't real.

the sacrifice was good for us in every way
we are better for it
we should be grateful

                                      We are great
                                            Not because we say we are
                                    We say we are
                                        Because we are

We must mop these shadows away.
We have no choice in this.
If we are culpable
  through laziness, smug indifference
  to the circumstances of others,
we admit

all that should be rectified -
but it's a separate matter.

>There's no way to ignore
>people kamikaze willing
>   to strike at you.
>it forces a sober evaluation
>(a majority swings to the hawkish).

>Prudence dictates extermination
>   radical surgery – extirpation
>   every adherent expunged
>   the indoctrinators
>   the volunteers
>   the contributors
>We can't be safe otherwise.

This won't be justice in the preferred sense,
there will be unavoidable 'collateral damage'.
We don't have the margin for certainty.
Or time to allow the changes maturation brings,
when youthful vehemence gets beached by wisdom;
narrow self-centeredness is shed, naturally gives way
to the wider recognition of the equality of others.
Regretfully we must reap the zealous and gullible.

>Sometimes even the young must chose their fate.
>between what is popular with their group
>   even be it murder and martydom
>or the sensible/responsible
>   an occupation
>   a real life.

Another discovery in our favor,
though capable of plotting,
the attackers turn out to be
    incredibly narrow sappers,
with no human perspective or fellow feeling.

The surprising gift – that noble savages still exist,
with the admixture of strict religious fanaticism.
They're almost too perfect to be real
scary slaves keen to obey - to sacrifice themselves
they're the dream burnt offering.

And the distraction has a benefit we won't mention
   allowing us to postpone indefinitely
answering how we've failed
to heed any of the injunctions of Jesus.
   To love those we hate
   (we're not allowed to hate anyone).
   To share our wealth.
   Never exploit others.
   Turn away from any violence
     - to be absolute pacifists.
   Spend our lives purifying ourselves,
     serving others,
     transcending the selfish.
Teachings that have always resonated
as our highest ideals, and deepest truths,
yet are impossible to follow.
Maybe this is the cavity in our core.
Half out of weakness, attachment, cowardice;
half because we simply don't agree with Jesus
that the material world
and all the powers that rule it, are inherently evil.
We've set out to master it.
  There are of course clergy who will fudge
   that this isn't what Jesus held,
  but you can take them all
  and roll them down the hill
  for they are as worthless as rocks.
      'The first shall be last,
       the last shall be first'
       is not so inspiriting
       when you are the first.

Were the trade towers a boast of dominance?
Can we say we really didn't mean them that way,
We weren't paying attention?

Still was it right for them to kill civilians?

> *Do you want to play biological warfare?*
> *Who do you think will win?*
> *We will kill you all*
>   *every man, woman and child.*

> *Do you want to play nuclear warfare?*
> *Who do you think will win?*
> *We will kill you all*
>   *every man, woman and child.*

For forty years we stood in a death duel
pistols cocked, pointed at our heads
while mind-numbing numbers ran
and psychopaths ran the game.
Megatonnonage, throw weights, multiple warheads,
all of it beyond comprehension
  endangering all living organisms on the earth
clinically insane
    (that's the kind of leaders we had)
Yes God in His mercy saved us.
How could the worms wearing rags
think we could be intimidated by them?
People who know nothing.
A race that rejected science.
    We will churn you into dust for the whirlwind
      to coat your mountains and deserts.
    You don't fear our power
    because you're willfully ignorant and lack imagination.
    You think of death as individual.
    But we understand kill or be killed.
    Annihilation is in our bones.

Go ask the American Indians
   - if you can find any -
We will see whose side God is on

You will be a people that once existed.

          We will blame them for everything we do
             for everything that ensues
          great slaughters
          government Security/Intelligence
          non-stop surveillance
          registering every person alive -
            DNA and computers.

              We must know about you my brother
                  or you will die
              We must know everything about you
                  or surely you will die

If we were ignorant
if we were complacent
if we lacked discernment
maybe we will learn a lesson.
    You will perish.

As long as we don't say
 (and avoid thinking)
these are lesser lives we are scrapping,
we will be free to pursue this course.

          They have passed this judgment on themselves.
          They cannot accept us as we are
            so they no longer belong.
          We are more of this age.

Those who have crossed us
are closer to the lightless Night
than they can suspect

Thank you God
   for giving us an enemy.
Thank you God
   for our supremacy.
The power and understanding
that allows us to dissolve our foes.
Acknowledging the perfection of Your Creation
fulfilling the part You have deigned to give us,
     We vow to correct
       any deviation in ourselves
       and any large deviations in the world.

The Girl I Should Have Married

I think of the many nice girls who liked me.
    I was a nice boy.
I remember one girl I sat next to
in a high school class
ironed white blouse, erect posture
always shone a smile on me.
Why didn't I go that way?
They would have forgiven much

maybe there was a selection I didn't know about
    or fate – I somehow intuited

When I was young I valued intellect too highly
    sometimes quick is surface
    and slow can hide inarticulate depth.
Feminine positioning can be difficult to follow
    if its felt
    more than thought.
Forcing verbalization is a losing proposition.
I've witnessed wives lose every argument
on particulars, on reasoning,
to husbands they'd one day discard,
yet in hindsight
their attitude and values were right.

    Love
the ideal relationship
to share, to be honest about everything,
You, your spouse, completely open
over years
    naturally
        gradually
each knowing the other thoroughly.
The fear would be
that later on you realize
    she misses a lot

And that it would bother you.
There cannot be blame
for what a person can't apprehend.
So you would be stuck.
Which is not to say there wouldn't be love
of the familiar-shared-life-attachment sort.
It just wouldn't be the ideal:
of Two   close together
sharing everything   on the journey

Besides the excitement, which is natural
   the nervousness
     fear of a faux pas you couldn't recover from
     or not measuring up physically,
underneath there was this deeper fear
of embarking on a life, a commitment
that in time you'd regard as a trap,
one you could never free yourself from.

                More than finding yesterday's prettiness
                    had worn away -
        If everything else was right
        that could be taken in stride
          a natural development.
        The greater fear would be to discover
        that the real person underneath
        was so much less than you'd supposed
        that your love collapses proportionately.
        Secretly the bond losing its sacredness,
        a change you could never acknowledge
        as your life becomes a chore.
            to be left on a cold grey beach
            watching the tide pull away

    There was a particular image
    imaginary scenario
    that scared me
    of marriage before success,

       to be sentenced
       confined to a small plastic apartment
       a generic wife pursuing nagging me
       about various personal shortcomings
           inadequacies and work failures
       - all of them true -
       with no garden to escape to
           caged there
       sinking denouement.
       (Since success never came…)

    The cure for wanting me
    is getting me

There was an exceptional woman
really wonderful in every way
Gorgeous, deep, sharp, moral,
Spiritual
Sensual
   with a sense of humor,
      Truly everything
and she liked me
     poor as I was.

But she had been married to a friend
and the more I told myself
that that wasn't relevant
the more it became
the only thing I dwelt on.
(They had had a child.)

On top of everything else was a fear
  - should it turn out to be a mistake -
that if I ever hurt a woman like that
I would never be able to forgive myself.

               I think I was a born romantic.
               My first crush occurred in the 2nd grade.

                    Bertha Baca
                        her beauty
                        the way she moved
                    her sweet reaction to everything
                I was swept away, enraptured.
                I never said anything.
                But I made sure I sat behind her,
                    to get near her.
                Studied her two blonde braids
                the skin on her slender arms
                    with the lightest fuzz.
                I wonder if she noticed I was besotted.

I learned too late
never have anything to do with Art girls.
though it looked like I belonged
    appreciation of the aesthetic
    foreign films
    hip music
searching
    rejecting conformity
sharing the pressure to be creative
    my blank white sheet of paper
    their blank stretched canvas

It wasn't them – it was me
whose exterior deceived
I looked bohemian
but underneath was wholly conventional
        marriage
        monogamy
        children

To Art eyes
people in the world
each a center to themself
exist as intriguing objects - bodies
interestingly different.

How can one argue?
in some sense this is true
What follows though is a preference,
a desire, to taste a fuller range,
dismissing vows and fidelity
as petty passé restrictions
imposed by bourgeoisie hypocrites.

You would be surprised how alert
they are to the danger of love
    the binding power it possesses
the threat it poses to end their freedom.
They chose instead
    loves for a season
a life of pronounced phases,
    over whole investment
    dull security
They won't foreclose opportunities
that may chance to come along.

When I was still young and impatient
though I thought myself mature,
full of such mad conceit – as being
hipper/smarter, carrying more inside,
that to think of it now makes me cringe,
I had extrapolated a prophetic puzzle
into a promise of success & perfect love.
Believing I had leverage on Providence,
heedless of the curse that such hubris
could bring down on my head,
when I fell for a fetching girl
I determined that this would be it.
Surely I had waited long enough.

Superior - I presumed I was in the know
    and she wasn't,
I would guide us
with Fate to rely on.

two meek sacrificial lambs

      I would have married her
      though it violated all my conditions
      I was nowhere - with no prospects.
      Even though younger, she was smarter.
      I got the comeuppance
         through heartbreak
           I deserved.

In all the world
I wonder if there could have been
two people less able to speak

The magnetism that pulled us together
   (a lot of it coming from sensing
   the mute suffering in the other)
contained magnetism's repulsive force
flipping us, always out of sync
exactly like poles
   that could never align.
Irresistibly attracted
yet every time we neared,
     pushed further apart.
So in a way it did turn out perfect
but in a cruel star-crossed way
  devastating

When to any sane person
it was clearly over
I still wouldn't accept it
endless strained imaginative denial

      If this is love who needs it?
      yet a life without that bond
         that fulfillment
         is shrivelment

When you're young
you're eager to sign up for experience
   (definitely including suffering.)
   From those you admire you've read
   that its needed to achieve depth,
   to master the complexities
       characters
       psychologies
       relationships
   to puzzle, plumb, and untangle;
   to live in the world of Dostoevsky.

But in the end if there was a relationship
I never want to spend another second
   thinking about -
Let it diminish me as a writer!
   I will sign an affidavit.
      I will waive everything.
         I'll run away.

Give me simple and apparent
   Eating a carrot
Just sitting. Staring

     May she always preserve her refined tastes
     Let her keep the belief
     I suppose she has
     in the abundance of love
     any night one may encounter a great love
     any day something new could arrive…

         Why should we be chained
          by the mistakes of youth?

     How do people come to decide
     I could spend my life with this person(?)

> Is the emotion so strong
> 	doubts are ignored or outvoted
> 'I exist now for _____.
> If change is required I will.'

Isn't love a tree planted for keeps?

> To accept
> be grateful
> see – embrace what you've been given
> work at what you have, nurture
> 	allow it to grow

I always felt it wasn't in me
to take on raising someone else's child.
Even (to be horribly honest) to adopt.
I have genuine admiration for the confident men
who shoulder these challenges and responsibilities.
An old timer I respected
  (he and his wife were raising a hyper grandson)
said it was natural to love a child.
I accept that as true.
   Even as a child I recognized
  my partiality to children and the old.
But I always feared the possibility
in actual irreversible circumstances
of finding you couldn't pull it off.
The love for a biological child
clearly exceeding that for an adopted or step.

Is it terrible to know yourself?

> Sometimes a girl or woman
> would suddenly focus on you,
> coyly draw you closer,
> obviously turning the charm up.
> You were flattered to be thought worthy,

    pleased to be seduced.
Later however
maybe reflecting on their act's artificiality
    was it right?
    was it real?
    would the persona be too hard to keep up?
they decide, overriding their feelings for you,
    and they did have some,
that they must wrap up this mistake/fraud.
You have no say in the matter. You never did.
You were picked
Now you're dropped.

In my experience
admittedly limited
women have been extraordinarily sensitive,
    kind and considerate
careful not to crush my feelings or confidence.
None ever said,
    'You have no future.'
    'I don't find you attractive.'
    'You're sexually inadequate.'
I had to figure it all out on my own
        afterwards

        A woman you glimpse one day
            in a used bookstore
        checking on titles
            in sections you like,
        her hair cropped chopped short
        equally divided between poorly bleached
        and brunette roots
        her attitude seeming to be 'I could care less'
        no makeup
        And you muse
        there is someone who would be honest
            no games
        obviously intelligent

        She'd be a merciless critic of my writing
        - but that's not all bad.
        of course in her sour moods
          she'd cut me to ribbons
        lashing out – scapegoating,
        and she'd have the ability to really hurt
        because she'd know, intimately,
          where all my vulnerabilities lay.
        As she's an unknown
        it's easy to fantasize anything.

Memory
   A good daughter of a religious family
In such a union there could be reliance
an enclosed love
    for both
that could grow
A decision definitely made forever.
You would have been committed
    and you'd have known it
No looking back
but maybe all to the good
      children

I don't deserve happiness

      Old bachelors are just as fussy as spinsters
        just as set in their odd ways.
      I'm totally eccentric
      I have clothes to take morning walks in
      clothes for public business
      clothes for socializing
      comfortable clothes for mornings and nights,
      and if I had money I'd have dress clothes,
      so there'd be a whole other set to juggle.
      I'm changing clothes all day long.
      And I often bathe a couple of times
      because I must be clean for clean clothes.

Children don't miss these proclivities,
"Uncle Eric's always showering."

It used to bother me,
the gossip one endures if not 'attached'.
People who don't even know your name
    guessing that you're probably gay.
Now I find these misappraisals amusing,
and the fact that I had ever been so sensitive
seems touching. I was a better person then.
I've moved from somewhat gay-phobic
    to elitist. Morally not an advance.
But it's hard not to feel contempt.
Most people (or should I say Americans?)
regard the life of the mind - and the spirit -
    as an incomprehensible occupation.
As human language must be to a parakeet.
The parakeet notices your eyes are fixed on it,
it hears the speech from your throat and mouth,
    - after all it can make noises too -
but it has no way of knowing that each word
    is an abstract signifier,
or that they can join together on a subject,
    possibly not even a visible subject.
So the average person regards the meditative
    with dismissive bewilderment
as distracted fools overly involved in nonsense,
    wasting their time on airy questions
with no substance, relevance or consequence.

I always assumed I'd be a good husband
I was pretty confident I'd be a good father
    My father was

It isn't until unwittingly you cross
some invisible boundary of age
that you realize the drift that's ahold of you.
How set you are in your ways

your fear-reaction to the prospect of risk,
    to taxing emotions
    to the boring repetitions of dialogue
    daily hassles.
Remembering you didn't do well with jealousy.
Fearing that drama's turn – discovery of betrayal
    the falling heart
  the cold blow. Dwelling in dark loss.

Reconciliation to a cool life instead
    safer   acceptable

        One shouldn't regret - ever - falling in love

            I was born a daydreamer
            There's nothing I can do about that
            But I want to die free of illusion

the limit

reaching the limit
a certain loose freedom came
placed
in the world
a particular life
the mundane circumstances of that life,
you finally exert your will

    a stretch of country road
    'the middle of nowhere'
        the quiet
    the warmed asphalt of summer
    in an odd mood
    you feel free to stray aimlessly
    a meandering weaving walk
    to violate the middle stripe's
    ruled division of the road
    in an amusing liberty
        it's a strange development
        that giving up
        frees one from care
            a relieved exhilaration

shorn of any regret
of blaming others
pushed to cast away all hope
    move on
    be over all this involving nonsense
everything of the past can stay with this sordid world.
        arms outstretched in welcoming
            ready for the real

I wish nothing hurt
but everything hurts

ORIGINAL

    threshold of something
the leaning imbalance
      you move to right yourself
the continuing almost-the-moment

unkempt farm
     strewn autumn
when colors in the world
   flowers showing the way
      wizen

a tethered animal's limited circle

freighted with a years engrossment
the monopolizing of daily demands
    tempered by exhaustion
only a surface ripple of apprehension
as a cool wind sends towards you
    purplish stacked stormclouds threatening
the last yield out there
a field of new mown hay
    lying vulnerable
Before the sublime beauty of the vast vista
   I can't stir
if the hay spoils it spoils.
If I have no money I have no money.
at this moment there's rapture
and the knowledge that I should be concerned
   only makes me smile.
All I want is to be part of it
   a betrothed love of the world
   a coming to terms with life

I imagine a call going out from here
   this place   this time
in a way to mark it as mine

TRANSLATION

    verge vertigo
teetering temporal fulcrum
the present is present at all times.
Autumn's pallid pastoral
    dessicated flora
the annual weakening to die dormant
provokes our own lapse
    negligent laxity
willfully letting the farm go
I study the colors fade
    plantforms decay
Blown in by a strong wind
vengeful stormclouds boil
threatening the last crop -
    mown hay
lying where it was cut.
this prospect: forfeiture of a years labor
Paralyzed by the visual beauty
I let go of that now remote concern
to 'realize full market value',
Hypnotized by the sublime's lull
have I completely cashiered care?
Rustic regions are the last strongholds
of old religions
    and old superstitions.
The dog yaps at nothing
to earn credit for doing its job,
but running in one direction
it ends collared up at the stake.

You can dwell on the hunching caterpillar
  (a pest) or the beauty in the butterfly.

To name this space and time,
inimical to everything urban and fashionable,

[Original cont.]

    the pain
      as by spokes
   shed now
     like a coat

I looked up one day
and noticed I loved you

Miracle with eyes.

How odd to think of a human being

I don't really know why
   - I have a lot of theories –
I love you

it's more important that she be happy
than that she be with me
and maybe she is happy

if things have gone astray because
   subconsciously
I always feel unready
Yet what would stop me
should the Golden Door open?

    Collaging words
      in tribute
    Will you accept?

scene: giant antique urns
to suggest a long ago past.
I am glad it is past

[Translation cont.]

      rack of pain – sensate rim
         when the load presses to the road
      turning spoke piercing crucifixion
      centurions casting lots for the garment.

I simply looked at you one day
and the recognition came
I had begun to love you unawares

    Idol with jewel eyes
the very incongruity that
a 'mere mortal' should have
    such magnetic power
reflective jumble of possible reasons
    guesses and hypotheticals
without a conclusion.
Fibrillation at the hint of rejection
shuffling verses together hastily
clumsy condensed collation of an obsession.
    Are the wretched distortions
    only phantoms I've imagined?
Did I create them simply to stall,
because I feel unprepared,
    ill-equipped, for good fortune?
Yet – should you chose to surprise me –
I promise you'll witness
    the birth of great joy.
stage scene: shopworn props and set
    left out, too late now,
    they must remain as the finale plays.
Resignation.

I never quite made it to life
I was too smart
too smart to risk doing it
to live

Reconceiving

having accidentally thrown away
   or misplaced
the draft you'd developed   teased out,
a formulation you took some pride in,
you're obliged to return, try to reconnect
with the inspiration that engendered it.

                while the separating time
                risks breaks and losses
                the interval also provides a chance
                in going back
                to mentally reencounter fresh
                the original conception
                          nature
                          essence
                remember what the context actually was,
                the impression's true direction and flavor.

Like the attempt to solve
- or at least grasp the contents -
of an odd but compelling dream,
with its jumble of emotions
perplexities and discrepancies;
as you recall the connections
      precedents
   label what you think was represented
trying to recall what you felt at each turn
   (sometimes its only the emotion that links,
   an association irrational - or a blend).
When awake, confident that you've shed,
   left that strange movie behind,
and are merely reviewing what was shown;
yet, while we're not conscious of this,
the effects aren't completely gone,
we're still in touch with the dream realm.

The descriptions and identifications
we casually apply, are informed and telling,
indicating the right reference and relation,
　　the gist of the action.
Though you assume you've emerged
　　you're still partway lingering
in that charmed air under the dome.

The attempt to put yourself back
to remember how the inspiration first hit you
so you can re-experience it again
　　whole and fresh
　　　How it struck - the sensation
　　　What seemed most important
　　　　nuances and directions
　　　　the Meaning that inhered

　　　　　　As you engage in this, your high estimate
　　　　　　　of that missing version pops
　　　　　　　you see its deviance
　　　　　　　and its jerrybuilt hodgepodge form.
　　　　　The poem had become its own product.
　　　　　The writing had begun to expand on itself,
　　　　　　words, phrasing, concepts,
　　　　　growing in the pursuit of a well-made poem
　　　　　no longer centered on the original subject
　　　　　　but this quite separate accreting self.
　　　　　Allowing cleverness to aggregate its own thing
　　　　　　no wonder it ended misshaped.
　　　　　No wonder you lost the enthusiasm to finish,
　　　　　　you'd lost contact with the source.

　　　　　　　Inspiration should be more than a start.
　　　　　　　When things go right
　　　　　　　the impression/image/feeling/energy
　　　　　　　　makes a persisting contribution
　　　　　　　　as a guide to the writing.

The loss had been inadvertent,
yet it turned out for the best.
Required to go back
(something we should do voluntarily)
the break allowed us to catch
    how far we'd strayed,
the chance to recreate
in a second effort
    something more faithful
        truer

The child
as an adult
always disappoints

a peculiar prophecy
(coming true / not coming true)
a strange fate

Confessing to an odd mind, an odd life,
professing an unusual relationship
   to 'the ground of being' [Tillich]
     I played it wrong.
I think of it as true and must record it as best as I can,
yet I fear the reaction:
   "You know that poet I told you I was reading?
   Yeah, turns out he's nuts. Really really nuts."

      In the beginning (among primary conditions)
         was Test
      And it was hard   It had to be hard

FATE

              It was a trick – from beginning to end
                though it would be incorrect
                   to say it was only a trick

I'm sorry World
I fell into my problems

I. History

Brace yourself, a (thoughts-words) prophecy
hung over my whole adult life.
For whatever reason the Absolute decided to lay it on me
when I was 20 years old, holed up in the medina of Tangiers.
It was 1968. I had hitchhiked through Europe.
I hadn't been prepared for how lushly beautiful
    southern France was.
Spain became more of an adventure.
(I should admit I was impressed
that all of Franco's guards had machine guns.)
The Youth Hostel in Madrid had bedbugs
   but it was worth seeing the Prado.
I was surprised at how big the Goyas actually were
- and for some reason it did make a difference.
I didn't eat much. I existed on warmed sugared milk.
   It was cheap and I discovered I really liked it.
Posters of bullfights, some upcoming, many past.
One night I was looking up at the stars when I fell asleep
awakened predawn by loud raindrops getting through
my sleeping bag. Too soaked, I had to abandon it.
Picturesque country, huge rectangular houses.
I got dropped off in the middle of nowhere
women all in black.
a man walking past with rabbits hanging from a stick.
I felt I could be back several centuries.
No rides.
It was coldest longest night I'd ever shivered through.
I couldn't sleep because I had to keep moving
   Spain - in summer.
I arrived in Malaga at sunset and it was like a dream,
colored lights and people on the boulevard
a beautiful woman carrying an unreal bowl of fruit.
A gay Englishman gave me a lift to Gibraltar.
At the time there was contention over its ownership.
He assured me how quickly British armed forces
would rout the Spanish if it ever came to fighting.

As to the prophecy
all these years later I don't remember if I was stoned,
but since I had gone to Tangiers
    famous as a destination for writers
to get stoned, in order to have a breakthrough,
it would seem likely.
Incidentally it never bothered me one way or the other.
I knew outside the West most traditional cultures
used an intoxicant to make contact with the spiritual sphere.

I don't have anything for or against the occult,
but I never regarded my experiences that way;
not as psychic encounters, mediumship, or spiritualism.
It was just God.
Since people understand God so differently
I will digress here to make clear my meaning.
Absolute, God, Providence, the Whole, to me its the same entity.
In my opinion all religions fail because of doctrine.
And its not their fault - they have to have doctrines,
otherwise people will go off on their own eccentric tangents;
    politically and theologically.
Another handicap is the tenet religions are obliged to hold
    that the Spirit can't grow.
The deity must be omniscient and omnipotent at a religion's birth
and this isn't simply to impose maximum awe,
it comes from a reasonable fear, since religions have a date of origin,
    as knowledge and societies change and progress
the relevance of old revelations and rules will be called into question.
And competition dictates that *our* religion, indeed our sect,
    is the only one with the real Truth.
Accordingly our faith receives special Divine approval.
Being favored thus blends in with a tendency in the West,
    cancelling all the advantages monotheism may have bestowed,
of making God a personification. Supremely powerful but a person.
It isn't true that only polytheists and animists personify,
    monotheists slide into it all the time.

Confront a Christian, Muslim, or Jew, and they'll deny this.
But their disavowal is meaningless.
As soon as they're not challenged they'll lapse back into that mindset.
Its automatic. Maybe it's the limits of human imagination.
So I want you to know that if I do employ 'He',
   its only due to the constraints of language.
Using the singular One to connote all, is fine.
Also the plural We, to denote the collective spirit.
And you could say 'It' which must be technically correct,
   helpful if you're attacking the error of personification,
   and seems suitable if what is discussed is particularly merciless.
Otherwise though, ironically, I feel its too inhuman.
I know that seems like a contradiction to my assertion;
but if the Absolute includes everything, and it does,
and if its ruled by living consciousness, and I believe it is,
then since humans are the most self-conscious of all the living
   (I don't believe in UFOs or extraterrestrials)
the godhead's ruling consciousness would be primarily human.

> We can regret the hatred that comes out of religions
>   but its quite natural.
> Even with their stilted doctrines its less religions' fault,
>   due more to human limitations.
> That guy across the river believes differently than me.
> His very existence is disturbing.
>   It threatens the peace and firmness of my belief.
> I need to see him not simply as ignorantly mistaken,
>   but as part of a group who couldn't grasp
> or achieve the higher good.
> Who have a weakness liable to be deceived by evil.
> We look down on Sunnis and Shias killing each other
> yet for centuries Catholics and Protestants
>   murdered each other in the name of a pacifist.
> So we can regret the hatred that arises from religion
>   but its like lamenting the weather.

Born into a radical family, an enemy of the 'system',
one creates a covert identity

that balances an elitist's awareness of the rigging
with a willed emotional solidarity with the exploited
   (but brainwashed) 'masses'.
Pretty difficult, but I think I pulled it off passably well.
So I had that background to help me
accommodate and assimilate my unusual experiences.
I didn't regard myself as abnormal.
The mystical feeling was constant
   so one stopped thinking about it.
The experiences that were odd by any definition
   happened so rarely
that they too were not in daily consciousness.
Since most of my life was normal I thought I was.
And one note - this wasn't ironclad –
with the prophecy apparently one of the exceptions,
   usually there was a distinct divide
between the supernatural (and the mystical),
and whatever you might experience via drugs.
I haven't taken anything psychotropic in a quarter century
but I remember this because when I was high
I would often wonder why there wasn't an overlap.
Another thing I should make clear from the outset
is that all these phenomena (excluding the mystical)
violated my theology. This was true from the beginning.
I accepted - and accept now - that what was reported in the past:
Old Testament prophecies, Jesus's healings, et cetera, did happen.
We don't know the veracity of any particular miracle,
   but I believe what we call the supernatural did occur.
Humanity has been essentially the same for a long time,
but the time period does matter. What is allowable changes.
I don't buy the denigration of our ancestors
as superstitious fools recording nonsense.
I think the rules of reality were different
in particular locales, depending on what was needed
and what those concerned believed.
My problem was that though I accepted participation
by the Absolute as even optimal 'way back when',
that curtain had come down several centuries ago.

Once upon a time gods – even God
had demanded animal sacrifices.
We grew beyond that. There is a spiritual evolution
   not just Nature's physical evolution.
The concept is that humanity learns, grows up,
   takes on full adult responsibility.
I don't think in the East they have any problem - in principle,
with latter day encounters with manifestations of the Divine.
However in the West all agree that it can't happen.
Since, for them, they've not only cast God as a person,
but as a stern authoritarian Patriarch 'laying down the law'
(each in their particular scriptures), with an obey or else attitude:
   'I've told you all. That's it. I'm not going to repeat myself.'
the silence after is explained – every truth has been covered.
None of that discipline nonsense was my problem.
I believed playacting as if God was an outside entity
was no longer appropriate or supportable.
And not just for enlightened human beings -
the mischaracterization was no longer acceptable to the Whole.
So how to explain the violations I kept experiencing?
When I was a young egotist I could flatter myself that
God could interact with me because I was special, an exception.
Existing on such a high level it had nothing to do with others.
Later I would realize it was more a case of someone
so screwed-up that if the Absolute didn't intervene
there would have been a dead animal on the ground.
   An example of 'non-survival of the unfittest'.

The expression, 'You asked for it' could apply,
especially if being lost can be seen
as calling for intervention.
Before I started hitchhiking,
I stayed in Belgium, and then London,
finishing up a novel I'd started when I was 16.
It turned out to be juvenilia, but I didn't know that then.
I mailed it back to the U.S. from England
and partly wondered if I hadn't done my job
   (as in 'Can I go now?')

The novel could have been interpreted as a plea for help,
   and I can't say for sure I wasn't aware of that.

I'd had enigmatic lines given to me before,
often containing a prophetic component,
but this was one long spiel, full of 'till's,
riddles, swinging lines, and packed words.
Via intuition-thought the whole thrust blatantly
   laid out this is what is going to befall you.
It balanced rewards and threats,
and had the conditional form required of such forecasts.
   [I've never approved of rhyme,
   with an exception for song lyrics
   where the echoing is in service to music.
   Rhyme – never suitable for English,
   and meter, subvert any poem;
   and for a century now have sabotaged
      the embodiment of anything organic,
      or the hope of reaching the serious.
   Yet Providence will occasionally still rely
   on mnemonic hooks, ones you can't shake.]
I assumed I had to prove my worth,
but was fairly confident I could.
This supposedly wasn't what I'd come to Tangiers for,
I had been searching for universal answers,
   not a roadmap concerning my personal fate.
But I was surprised, not unhappy. It seemed like a gift
to have Providence roll out your whole life,
even if in complicated riddles.
The promise (or so I deduced) was blissful happiness;
meaning both artistic success and true love.
I not only made up this interpretation,
   I also gave it a sequence: love first, then success.
Not based on anything in the prophecy, only reasoning
that Providence, knowing my mistrustful nature,
   would want the love to come first,
   so I'd have no grounds to suspect
      that my success had been the real appeal.

I felt, given enough time - and boy was I given enough time –
I could untangle the riddles, connect significances
   in the way they were meant to be ordered.
Multiple meanings didn't phase me.
I thought dream interpretation would help locate keys,
   meanings that intersect through puns,
   strainings that were giveaways as important.
Reading Kabbalah esoterica would finally pay a dividend:
   2 designating the true love,
   beth, the feminine, home-housing.
   (Aleph was 1, the masculine, active agent.)
But I didn't stop with that, I ran everything:
   'to see', 'two see', 2 c's, everything cc stands for,
      even the speed of light squared.

Though I have a patent pending on lost,
in some respects I was less naïve than your average fool.
I had read my Herodotus.
I knew the tricks and traps oracles could set,
the double meanings in the wording of a prophecy
   that if not caught
might encourage a disastrous assumption.
Most famously King Croesus of Lydia asking at Delphi,
   should he go ahead and attack Cyrus and Persia?
Told that if he did a great empire would be destroyed;
he didn't stop to ask himself, could that empire be mine?
He had made unprecedented sacrifices and donations,
he had every reason to feel sure of the gods' favor.
According to Herodotus he didn't understand
that no one, not even the gods, can alter or escape fate.

   Out of the fear that it might prove phantasmal
   I wasn't going to let the prophecy rule my life.
   Yet I believe Providence planted it when it did,
   at the onset of adult life, deliberately,
   so I'd never be entirely free of its influence.
   I'm trying hard to avoid the cliché of 'haunted',
      and truly I don't feel that term applies,

but it was always back there:
    'Is this part of the prophecy?'
    'This girl is equivocal – so it can't be her.'

I will try to relate my version of my meanderings,
which turned into a 40 year slog through the desert
constantly on the lookout for secret signs,
hope raised whenever a possible reference was glimpsed
    Was that a mirage -
    or a real marker - there to encourage?
    Have I overlooked something?
    Am I reading it right - or imagining?
    horizon after horizon approaching then receding,
        belief wearing thin

Feel free to laugh at this chronicle.
To me its tragic
but I know how ludicrous it appears.
I don't count the first 3 ½ years,
because I tried to bend the prophecy to fit my will.
I want you to know though
that I did suffer for this idiotic hubris.
Anyway because of this I start my count from 1971,
and maybe it should even be a little later, I don't know.

Events would occur – key words triggered.
The first big one was the acronym CREEP,
    the Committee to Re-Elect the President.
The investigation of their activities – Watergate,
    would spell doom for Nixon,
whose downfall of course I cheered.
I got my hopes up. Now its all going to kick in.
Nothing.

Then a decade later, the FREEZE movement arose.
Anti-nuclear, also with which I was in full sympathy,
and again I thought: now its going to actualize.
But nothing happened.

Its not that these couldn't have been incidental signs.
    They probably were.
    The Absolute can do anything it wants;
       multiple uses/meanings are the rule, not the exception.
But as principals, time would show, they weren't.
My next hunches would be just as off,
and elaborating 'freeze' I proceeded to make an error
    so grave I probably never recovered.
It was the neatness of my solution that was seductive.
On the surface temporal level, I decided it indicated
one particular gardener's freeze,
    either the last freeze before the growing season,
    or the first freeze that marks its end.
This was the specific time when *whatever* would start.
At a higher level it meant God had placed a hold
    on my career (a grandiose term for such a nullity)
    until that time commenced.
And lastly, at the highest level, it was a reassurance;
'creep' and 'freeze' working together
    to reinforce the message
that while yes the journey was a long one,
when I reached the promised land
time would seem to slow or stop.
Believing I had successfully tied it all up
I stopped looking for other applications.
So much time then passed, with nothing happening,
that like my unopposed true love scenario,
my solution seemed to solidify merely by existing.
I can't argue that otherwise I would have caught on,
but when you think you already possess the answer,
    a correct - and comprehensive – resolution,
you aren't alert, and when there is a change,
the odds are good you'll miss its significance.

I don't want to overstate my convictions,
portraying them as more resolute than they were,
and not give doubt equal time.

Most of this period was dominated by uncertainty.
On the other hand I was always ready
should I see the prophecy coming true
   to demonstrate my faith.

The problem, when you have an imagination like mine,
   with so many years to fill,
is that you start constructing the 'likely' scenario.
Making conjectures that harmonize with each other,
   as well as with the original cryptic codex.
Unfortunately the extrapolations became - in my mind -
as firm as what was sent, which of course they weren't.
There's no one to question your deductions,
and until an event occurs that contradicts your story,
   it continues as part of a credible whole.
This was my scenario:
   When all the signs would lock & check out
   the true love would appear.
   The attraction would be immediate
     I would 'home in' on her
     She would 'home in' on me
   (ancillary to all this she would know,
   and naturally – favor - my writing;
   though I never explained exactly how
   she was supposed to come across it.)
   All of Nature would sing the chorus Yes.
   I would approach her and say,
     Look a long time ago I had this prophecy…
   It would strike her as very strange
     - since of course it is -
   but because she was the one
   it would resonate in her soul
   she would know (feel)
     it wasn't a line
     it wasn't a lie
   it was the organic truth.
   Destiny fulfilled   bliss.

The crucial transition in the prophecy
occurred with the requirement
   that I 'die in a flare'.
I imagined the kind of flare that's fired in the air
   signal for help I guess.
A metaphorical death that would swiftly occur.
To be followed I assumed
   by a metaphorical rebirth just as swift.
This is pretty funny - and/or pathetic,
but 20 years in found me pleading - prodding God,
'Hey its not possible to feel any deader than I do now.'
   I'm not kidding. For all the good it did me.
Even if you weren't a space cadet like me
most of the conjunctions alluded to in the prophecy
could only be apprehended after they happened.
I really believe that to be the case.
However the metaphorical death was the exception.
Its first instance was something I could have –
   and should have - anticipated.
I was caring for my father.
His decline was drawn out, its end unmistakable.
I'd heard how punishing the of lack of sleep could be,
but experiencing it as a loved one helplessly faltered
   took a staggering toll.
Yet what I came to see as the cause of my 'dying'
   wasn't exactly his death,
but the compounding realization in its wake
that even if I did 'make it' now at some point,
   my father would no longer be there to see it.
As I said I had all the time in the world to foresee this.
Why didn't I?
And why was it so crushing?
Its not like I don't believe in the next world – I do.
   Dad didn't.
And this would've meant more to me than to him.
He loved me, he was proud of me anyway.
   (Surprisingly, since he wasn't literary,
   he had been one of the few who appreciated

  a disjointed play I'd written.)
But he would have been elated at any success.
Prouder? I don't know - maybe a justification.

My father died on July 14th.
As a respite from grief
and a house full of reminders
I took Mom down to my sister's for a week,
to be surrounded by happy burgeoning life.
On the way back home we picked up Dad's ashes.
Shortly thereafter I saw this pure young beauty
and she inspired two lines that end this book
   "Sometimes good is good
    light is light".

 I know they seem like simplicity itself,
but that's part of what recommends them.
  If you don't write poetry
  you might not understand
  how hard it is to distill
  - capture an essence,
  choosing words that don't lead astray.
I didn't think anything about her
  except that I was grateful for the inspiration.
Pleased that as low as I was
I was still capable of seeing – feeling - writing.
I really liked the haiku-like succinctness of the lines,
  and also I must say their positive thrust.
It was only a couple days later that it occurred to me
wait a minute – I have died in a flare,
  and now I have an inspiration that ends
'light is light'. Maybe this is the key clue.
It started to make sense.
I understood why I could never discover the girl
  - she hadn't been born.
And if she was to perceive my dying in a flare
that had to wait for its cause – my father's death.
The corroborating sign I had searched for

turned out different than anything I'd contemplated.
Not solely by a flare's light, but the word 'light',
that she would inspire me to write.
And the very thrust and nature of the two lines
    was confirmative.
It was perfect in every way.
(Later I'd grasp another aspect of its perfection,
it braced Providence against complaint to riposte:
       This was *your* inspiration.
       Your selection. Yours all the way.)

She was the right type,
something like my first crush in the 2nd grade,
a skinny blonde girl.
But it was obvious she was conservative,
   not, as I expected, someone 'on my wave-length'.
I wouldn't be able to speak frankly
   to anyone in her family,
and she wouldn't be free to be unguarded
   with anyone in mine.
Yet this is the one hurdle I think I handled well.
If the Absolute wanted a cosmic marriage
   drawing together opposite sides
I could understand that goal - ideal,
   and was happy to go along with it.

More of a problem,
though I'd always expected child-bearing age,
was that this girl, though tall, looked awfully young.
There's a college at the county seat
   and I thought maybe she was enrolled there.
No, it turned out she was a high school student.
Not even a senior - a junior. 16 years old.
You can't even speak to a 16 year old.
   It's immoral.
So after one has given up,
the old dream materializes -
you think God has finally shown mercy,

>   your hopes rise from the cold ashes.
>> As swiftly as it manifests
>> you confront a wall surrounding it.

I tapped into the one talent I indisputably possess,
> an endless fount of self-pity.
As beautiful as the girl was
God had made me wait 35 years
only to give me someone too young to even speak to.
I pouted like the worst spoiled brat.
> (I'm sorry, but if after 35 years
> a surprise wrinkle like this - a late addition -
> if pouting for a few weeks is unacceptable,
>> then please just shoot me.)

When I pulled myself together
I gave myself a little pep talk:
> Look you've gone this far.
> What's a few more years?
> Now at least you know she exists.
Attempting to make sense of it
I decided God wanted an absolute test.
> Recognition of pure being by pure being.
> With no words - no persuasion.
> A proof of true love recognizing true love.
That's what I believed.
To this day I've never come up with a better alternative
(You're free to say the alternative is you're crazy.)

I quickly realized how wrong I'd been about 'you creep'.
It wasn't a verb at all, it was a noun.
I was going to be the perceived creep,
> a much older guy with a girl too young.
But I shrugged that off.
What do I care what outsiders think?
> if I'm blissfully happy with wife and family.
As time passed though
it wasn't just that she was too young

    she was too cold.
In my imagined scenario she came around immediately
    (of course she wasn't underage either).
It could have been when I found out she was only 16
    I went into total restraint;
and maybe that sent the wrong signal – as in no signal,
    for her to read and react to.
There were moments
when you thought you caught something
but you were never sure.
I told myself well look I was given the prophecy
so Providence meant for me to have this advantage
in knowing how things are going to turn out.
No matter how she might resist now
    she's destined to fall for me.
And I'd tell myself beautiful girls are
constantly attracting unwanted attention,
    they have to erect defenses.
Yet, many times I asked God,
    "Why the Ice Princess?"

It was as close to operating on pure blind faith
    as I am capable of.
And somewhere – in the midst of the five years
I did fall in love with her,
even though she stayed distant and aloof.
I couldn't to this day tell you why.
Was it obedience to God -
    I had been directed to this girl.
Was it because she really was my true love,
    so it was only natural?
Was it the combination of the two?
    I'll never be able to untangle it.

I don't want to create a biased picture,
this girl was warm and friendly to her friends.
And even with me there were exceptions.
The biggest one occurred one year at Christmas,

there was snow and ice so I was walking,
    carrying a medium sized turkey,
and she wished me a sweet "Merry Christmas".
I had walked on a ways before it hit me
    'Hey she was just sweet to me.'
But that shows you how unusual it was.

How do you gauge
when sufficient maturity has been achieved,
is there some tip off or rule?
She was an old young, but still…
I am proud of the fact that as far as I am aware
my behavior was always proper.
I never crossed any line.
I played everything by the book.
So even if all of this
turned out to be a big hallucination
    she was the wrong girl
    or there never was a right girl
I'd have nothing to apologize for,
as I'd never committed a transgression.

You'll be amused at what I came up with,
after enough time had passed and she was old enough
that the possibility of expressing how I felt existed;
and if done in a decorous way
    wouldn't violate law or morality.
I worked on the line for years
    and this is what I came up with:
"I think you're the most wonderful thing in Creation."
I was never happy with 'thing',
but I could never come up with a substitute
    that was inclusive enough.
I never had the opportunity or nerve to use it though.
She was always so defensive and standoffish,
I thought she might bite my head off,
or slam the door so tightly shut
    that I'd never be able to pry it open again.

Its beyond bizarre that all this would center
on the affections of a girl who was
   and who would remain – a stranger.

               Though I was romantic when young
               I disliked the immature, even twisted,
               Dante/Petrarch glorified pristine love,
                  an untouchable idealization.
               It didn't strike me as noble or tragic,
                  simply strained and ridiculous.
               This may reveal a dearth of sympathy,
                  no doubt there have been star-crossed loves,
                      doomed by circumstances.
               Yet I was suspicious of fancies
                  unnatural and unhealthy
               inflated to pass as transcendently sublime,
                  whose impossibility was part of their appeal.

Late, in a sort of subtle, not-too-subtle way,
she lets me overhear that she's found Mr. Right:
   "My life is so full."
Because I saw God conducting the entire show
my assessment was different than you'd expect.
   I thought, Okay, what we have here -
   at the same time as she's bouncing this off me,
   she's trying to convince herself:
      'I've found my future. Maybe. Have I?'
With lunatic confidence I told myself,
   God has actually revealed how it's going to go.
   You're just a little lost conservative girl
      trying to talk herself into some deviation.
   (It turned out the joke was on me.
      It was already too late.)
There was a lot of fault on my side.
Because I had the prophecy I waited.
To make sure. To have her show her hand first.

At some point I will have to face up
   to the unpleasant business
of revealing to you the last line of the prophecy,
and this is as good a spot as any.
I am worried you will overreact -
   i.e. use your own mind in deciding,
   not take it the way I want you to.
While nothing in this poem is anything
I ever planned to share publicly
my trepidation on this has another twist.
I fear even those who've made a good faith effort
   to stick with me this far,
seeing things as I saw them,
after I divulge this, will shake their heads
   and give up on me.
The last line (rhyming with 'creep') was:
   "*Man, you're in deep.*"
I can't blame you for thinking
   'Now we see why you withheld this.
     You weren't misled.
   You made up all the end-of-the-rainbow stuff
   when in fact you were warned
     your final predicament would be ominous.'
Allow me to tell you how I took it,
knowing this will come off as special pleading.
Yes I blew it off.
But the Absolute knew I'd blow it off,
   it was styled to be blown off.
My take on it, from the first (and ever after)
   was 'Tell me something I don't know.'
Politically I was born in deep, internal enemy,
   family - whole life - under surveillance.
   Who was a rat? Who might become one?
Even later, you can regard yourself
as a true Christian & a real American patriot,
that doesn't mean the secret police will
   (and given their conception of the state
     I'm not sure they were wrong.)

Beyond the political, as you read this book
you'll see that artistically, emotionally, spiritually,
I was dwelling at the bottom of the ocean.
Telling someone like that that he's 'in deep'
   will come off obvious and superfluous.
And like the maneuver that took my inspiration
   as the key in selecting the true love,
its 100% cover. That's how I saw it.
   A 'You were warned you'd be in deep.'
This doesn't excuse, once again, over-confidence,
   my not going back, revisiting an interpretation,
   or, as in this case, a dismissal of a warning.
Nor in any way to deny the rank stupidity
of grumbling for five years about an Ice Princess
   and not thinking of 'freeze'.

Anyway I didn't see her for awhile,
apparently she'd moved to the next town,
   where the college is.
Our local paper is a weekly
   and one day there it was,
      a birth announcement.
'This is **irrevocable**.' I'm a word person
and for some reason, at that moment
   irrevocable was the word.
As in you can't be the true love
and have a baby by someone else.
She could have fallen for someone,
even lived with a boyfriend for a period.
   But a baby – that tore it.
I felt God had sandbagged me. Seriously.
Set me up. All of this.
I'd been a good soldier, shown faith,
gone along with a conservative,
fallen in love, even though she was cold,
   and this slam ending was my reward.
God, with premeditation, had tricked me,
intentionally foisting a defective girl on me.

One interesting note at this juncture
considering all the doubt that had hung about,
was that the thought that she wasn't the one
   never came up.
Even though this would have seemed
like the right moment, things having gone awry.
No. The deeper me knew it was her.

      I've learned the hard way
         don't ever say
      'Well at least things can't get any worse'
        - wry humor as solace.
      When you do the floor opens up
      and you fall to a new level of hell
        you didn't know existed.

      If you had posed the quandary of
      a person in love
      with someone they couldn't accept
      I could have imagined it
        especially in some long ago past
          when a difference in religion,
          or social level,
          or an unfortunate scandal,
        dictated what was acceptable.
      Never that such a dilemma
      could possibly ensnare me.
      Yet now I saw God's strategy.
      When I fell in love
      the trap closed behind me.

If God wants to trick and trap you
   you will get tricked and trapped.
Doesn't matter if you can outsmart all of humanity,
   you can't outsmart God.
I had been set up and I knew it.
There had been no hint of a baby.
There had been no

'In the 4th year of your vigil
she will fall for another.
In the 5th year of your vigil
she will give birth to a child from this union.'
God knew I wouldn't even look at her.
I never expected a cake walk.
Along with the honor and privilege
I fully expected the burden of having to measure up.
    Well forget honor and privilege
        it was only burden.
Almost immediately I saw how wrong I'd been.
I'd assumed the test was faith and endurance
    spread over 40 years,
when in fact the crucial part
was rigged to come at the end.
And it was customized, aimed at my weakest traits:
my inability to forgive, my inability to trust.
Even a vow I didn't know was a violation,
    that I would never raise another's child.
I never thought unforgiving or mistrusting were good,
but I presumed individuals had the prerogative
to determine what they found personally acceptable.
I hadn't considered it a provocation,
    tantamount to setting a condition on the Absolute.
The truth is up until then I always figured
Providence, knowing all my faults,
    had taken me as I was.
Why not give me this test 40 years ago?
30 years ago? 20 years ago?
I would have failed whenever it was given.

    'Its somebody else.'

In the wake of being crushed
I got looks of sympathy
from some of the girls and women
who had been her co-workers in the past.
I'd never said anything to anybody

but I guess they caught me mooning after her,
and now saw through my act - beneath it
   to the stricken survivor struggling on.
Not a hint of contempt,
or even the look towards one who got
   a comeuppance he should have expected.
Though they had to see me as an older guy
forming an unrealistic crush on a young girl.
It was all compassion, goodness of heart.
So I don't know why
   as one who posits humiliation as good
      in putting ego back in its place,
it felt like a final too-much added on.
Maybe because it confirmed
   I had been destroyed
   and I was visible.

One thing I need to note
is that I bore the five years of cold
   sometimes perplexed,
   sometimes challenged – having doubts,
   questioning God on the purpose,
but finally accepting it as part of the trial.
I would tell myself to trust -
You were given the prophecy so you would know,
   you have this advantage, so lean on it.
Yet when it ended – her being cold
was immediately noted on the ledger.
Funny how it jumped - tolerated for five years,
then wham - added to the grievances side.

I had come to a fork in the road
   and it didn't matter which path I chose
rising behind and above each was Doom.
The first path was God makes mistakes.
This was only a hypothetical option
since I could never for a second believe it.
Those who have a strong view of free will

could argue Providence has to wait
    for us to make our decisions
and because of that there's a necessary contingency.
But I'm so far in the opposite predestination camp
    it would be preposterous for me to even pretend.
Nor as one who doesn't believe God makes mistakes
could I now append a complaint,
    "Except for me. He really blew it with me."

So I was left with: set up.
I spent that fall and winter very mad at God.
You don't need to tell me that's a marker of insanity,
    I knew it – even at the time.
Plus not believing God was a person
    only made it that much more absurd.
What explanation could I come up with?
There couldn't be a [personal] motive to 'get' me.

And there was the whole issue of gratitude.
A weight another soul would not have had,
    but I had to live with.
Not a small one either - an incredible debt,
    which I acknowledged in my head
    while feeling nothing in my heart.
This division had been true for years
    yet there was nothing I could do about it.
If you don't feel something
telling yourself you should doesn't make it happen.
I often thought (though how would I know?)
that there probably wasn't anyone in history
who had benefitted from more 'saves' than me,
and I lived at the wrong time for such interventions.
And I'm not referring to spiritual redemption,
I mean saving my physical body – life.
A long time ago
    the Absolute decided it couldn't trust me.
A couple years before the prophecy,
when I was 17,

I took LSD for the first time.
It was still legal. If it hadn't been
as a law-abiding son of a probation officer
I might not have been open to taking it.
It was reputed to make Buddhas – quickly.
The irony is that this was a good trip.
   (The second trip was a nightmare,
      as were many that followed.)
A friend and I each took a tab at his apartment,
with his Mother home, staying in the back portion.
As it starts your eyes dilate to an extreme.
I looked up at the old plaster around the chandelier
and it was a circle of bare showgirls' legs kicking.
I got immersed in this book of Van Gogh.
   At the time he and El Greco were my favorites.
   Eventually I tired of El Greco's sameness,
      though his spirituality was real.
   But my love for Van Gogh never diminished.
   You understood that all the swirls were right,
      including the ones in the sky.
   Schizophrenia has a mystical aspect,
   certainly Van Gogh's did. With the LSD
   you saw that nothing is solid, everything gives
   sways ripples, is in internal motion,
      in a way alive, almost breathing.
   I stared and stared at the 'church at Auvers'.
It was when I went to the bathroom
   that the unexpected occurred.
Your image in a mirror is strange -
   constantly moving, expressions shifting.
Suddenly, calmly, I would say dispassionately,
the idea culminated: you should kill yourself.
I had never had a suicidal thought before.
I need to relate this accurately.
I was high – and for the first time,
but it wasn't that I couldn't think properly.
   I was SuperConscious.
And it wasn't an evil spirit invading,

nor was it the result of a chemical chain-reaction
inside the physical body, upsetting its function.
It was more like a door opening to a room
    that had always been there,
though you'd never known, before that moment,
    that it was there. It was definitely you.
It had appraised everything
and very seriously counseled
    the best course was to give it all up and get out.
I agreed. It was the smooth concession of the truth
    of some self-evident realization;
something that had never occurred to you before,
but when it did
    you were instantly and completely persuaded.
What stopped me was the thought that his mother
would have to clean up all the blood,
    and I couldn't do that to her.
I always looked back on that as an example
of how consideration for others can save you.
The funny thing is if it'd just been my friend
    I wouldn't have cared.
I've always condemned suicide as morally wrong.
Its selfish - it hurts others; and its stupid -
we're only given one life. Don't throw it away.
Not that it isn't permissible for someone suffering
    from an incurable disease - or unending pain.
But otherwise its immoral - and yes cowardly.
I never wanted to hurt my family like that.
Still from that day forward I had to contend
with the attendance of that part of me, that voice,
and in times of despair, or depressions,
    as you would expect, its strength grew.
Yet, with one lapse, it never again had control.
The real effect only manifested
    in odd moments of danger
when the natural response would be to recoil.
Instead I would hold still,
    as if waiting to see what would happen.

Would the exit open?
As if that would make it okay,
   because then it would be fate's doing.
I have a wonderful capacity for denial,
and if you only do this once, who's to say,
you got caught off-guard, stunned, perplexed.
That can explain one instance of immobility.
Do this repeatedly and you don't need a shrink
   to see there's a pattern, and a problem.
The truth is I didn't correct the behavior,
   God started interfering.
That's what really happened.
So when I say my debt is immense
   I'm not being hyperbolic.
And when I speak of the gratitude
I know I owe
   that's all in my head
   with absolutely nothing in my heart,
you'll understand the guilt clouding about
and the proper context of viewing
   an idiot angry at God.

I knew some things. One of them was, no matter
how much God may have wanted to punish me
   – apparently pretty severely,
the girl selected had to have a great and holy soul.
There could be no getting around that.
God could never anoint someone who wasn't worthy.
She couldn't be Jane Doe picked at random
   out of the phonebook.
So I knew that.
And I knew that meant her soul must have told her:
   'Doesn't matter if he's old.
   Doesn't matter if he's poor
   - a writer who's never sold anything -
     he's the one.'
If she was Jane Doe picked at random of course
there would be no sense in anything that happened.

However, provided I'd read the signs right,
    and I was sure I had,
something like this must have occurred internally.
But her mind overruled her soul
    and it said, 'No way Jose.'

Let me interject an admittedly subjective observation,
but as someone who has always held
children and women above men,
    and I'm not just saying this,
I had the impression, long before these events,
that one area where men had an advantage
was in valuing the rareness of love.
Not the extreme example this poem's about,
the made for each other types – perfect fit -
I'm speaking of the more normal kind,
    with adjustments, and growth around each other.
In my view men (I'm not talking about fools
who don't realize they have better than they deserve;
or egoists too far into self to ever look outward)
appreciate the rareness of love more.
I know this isn't the commonly held view
    which sees women as the more romantic.
I don't think that's a contradiction actually.
A belief in love means imagining it could be better,
could arrive any time, from somewhere unexpected.

I was totally destroyed,
yet I had two responses that escaped,
    running crosswise to my devastation.
Even now it seems odd that they occurred.
One was a perception of symmetry.
I had been 20 when I received the prophecy.
If my math was correct, when she tore it up
    she would have been around 20.
Its a funny thing to have your mind go to
when you've just been annihilated,
    but I couldn't help it.

If you're like me, the idea/ideal of symmetry,
   the scientific principle of
     'entanglement',
is fascinating.
Like veins of a great balance made visible,
something we're usually unable to see,
   that reveal a harmony inside the whole.
   (If we're lucky we can feel it.)

The other reaction that diverged
from the situation and my state
   was an admiration of her will.
Though I judged over-riding your soul
to be bad, in this case disqualifying -
   and I didn't kid myself, her rejection of fate
   directly equated to a rejection of me -
I couldn't help but admire
   the assertion of will. The courage.
I think this must come from being the opposite.
Amusing because I appear to be a non-conformist,
I think because I was a hippie (sort of),
I was born into a politically radical family,
   and I seem to stubbornly go my own way.
But I've never had a choice on my bizarre course
and I'm as far from a rebel as one could imagine.
True if I don't get guidance on an idea
I may take it as a green light to act,
   which often ends disaster.
But if I get instructions I am this obedient dog.
A very apt example is at hand:
the title of this book and its (to follow) prose brother.
I considered possible titles as I wrote.
For the poetry I was leaning towards "Impressions".
I didn't get that far with the prose book,
but because the plan was to write different stories
   in a variety of forms
I was considering names that would connote a mix:
Miscellany, Spectrum, Sampler, Omnibus, like that.

Forget it. What has been selected is imparted
    (again not spoken – intuition thoughts).
They strike me as more like gag titles.
I'm sure they have some inscrutable deep meaning,
but I write satires and the piquant mirth
would seem more suitable to books of humor,
not for a writer's most serious works
    executed (presumably) in his prime.
The "Do You Know Who I Am?" struck me
as reprimand by some insufferable snob shopper
    demanding servile attendance from an employee.
The other is "You don't know me but…
which seems like an interfering interruption,
    the opening of a pitch to hawk something.
Obnoxious customer and pushy salesman,
    I guess that covers everything.
The weird thing was the Absolute had no preference
    about which title got stuck on which book.
That was left to me, which seemed rather odd.
Of course I am free to discard these titles
and select ones I feel
    are more elevated and appropriate.
There's nothing to stop me.
However you need to understand that option
    is strictly theoretical – air - not actual.
Rebellion is not really considered. Never has been.
That's why I say I'm a submissive dog.
Hence when I see someone who does diverge,
charting her own course, even at my cost,
I can't help but admire that independence.
I have never felt free, but with the prophecy
at the onset of adult consciousness,
though it took me a long time
to catch on to what had happened,
I got encased in a heavier coat of the determined.
    (Not saying God didn't have good reasons.)
42, or 43, years later to see the other half
at the onset of her adult consciousness

asserting control - freeing herself,
even if somewhat unconsciously,
how could someone like me
not admire such an exertion of will?

Right after I'd read the birth announcement
I did slip and blurt out to my sister
    "The girl God wanted me to marry
        just had a baby."
But my sister loves me.
She'll chalk it up as just be another weird thing
  . her weird brother believes.
Had she known of the age disparity
    she would not have approved.
Not on religious grounds, though she's Muslim.
Old religions come out of patriarchal societies
created and run by senior men in authority
who of course have a partiality to such matches.
Its her personal distaste for these relations
    which she sees as one sided and unnatural.

            You can label me credulous,
            I do believe in 'love at first sight',
            and I believe it can happen to one of a couple
            and the other might need some time. Maybe a lot.
            What I'm talking about isn't like that.
            This kind has to be a two way street. Has to be.
            Its impossible - absolutely impossible - for one
            to experience true love and not the other.
            It must be both.
            You don't have to agree with me on this
            but you must understand my conception.

When I say I was devastated I'm not exaggerating.
I did the whole 'God, why have you abandoned me?'
    I cringe to admit it now, but its true.
That fall/winter I think of as falling off a mountain,
striking rock shoulders three times on my way down

each impact a run-in with the girl.
Because it had been phrased 'a flare'
I assumed it was a singular event.
No such luck.
It did apply to that period leading up to '06
   the slow death, the wearing down,
   followed by the realization that even if I made it
   my father wouldn't be there
     writing the two lines
     seeing the 2
     being seen by the 2 too
all that – but it didn't stop there.
I'm the kind of person who frequently asks himself
   Did I really know what I presumably knew?
Especially in hindsight, after being surprised,
when it seemed I knew something, had it,
yet it was never properly assimilated;
its ramifications, simple prediction of function,
   overlooked, never developed.
This is how I view this -
beyond getting tricked by the phrasing.
If I'd really focused on 'die in a flare'
I should have understood I was the flare
and obviously the light engendered
   was from my burning.
The girl might be the good light
but the light coming from me
   would not be pain free.
Anyway five years of this drill
were going to come round again and again,
in sharper activations, in the nature of assaults.
Unlike the original, which I had awaited,
   hoped for - for so many years,
now I didn't want the light, to see and be seen by.
    But I was not to be spared.

The first happened as I was feeling upbeat,
   having just completed a good deed.

A handicapped friend had called
telling me she had to leave home
before she could coax her two kittens in.
Could I go to her house, find and lock them inside?
The mission was accomplished with surprising ease.
On the way home I decided to stop for eggs and sundry.
I turned around and there she was.
Baby in a pink basket perched atop a shopping cart.
Good looking young man, very All American.
I assumed he was the father
(but later figured out he must have been a brother).
It was a shock. And I fled immediately.
But nothing can excuse what I thought:
    'God has matched me with a big dumb animal.
       She's like one of the horses she loves.'
Simply horrible
(my response at the second run-in
   would be even more egregious.)
All I can say, as a person who takes pride
in his ability to control himself, in 'maintaining';
is that there are moments in all of our lives,
when you can't control your reactions.
You simply can't.
   You're not able to hide them either.
They just are what they are, you're stuck,
   there's nothing you can do about it.
I was thinking 'how do I get through this day?'
'How do I take the next breath?'
Of course I regret how I reacted,
but how do I say that wasn't me,
when it was me raw, without a skin.

The next time wasn't too long after the first.
It was morning, I was walking to the post office,
when suddenly she emerged from her car.
She gave me a look I had waited five years for:
   that she understood who we were.
Now she was giving it to me

with someone else's baby in the car.
I know you will think I imagined this
   but I didn't.
I had an even uglier thought
one word (rather like irrevocable)
   'Untouchable'.
My head turned away, eyes stayed on her,
that involuntary wary sidelong appraisal
you have towards someone who has burned you.
She registered the glance for what it was.
I hope you will take my word,
I am not some orthodox nut who goes around
   making Old Testament condemnations.
I don't even know anyone like that.
But again this was me. That was how I reacted.

Thankfully the third time
   was free of evil ugly thoughts.
It was more like I was a captured specimen
   pinned to a board.
For whatever reason the collector
had skipped anaesthetizing me to death
   I would die in good time
   fixed in place where I belonged.
I had gone to the next town,
where she had moved, to buy Christmas cards.
I was back in my car when I saw them.
This was the boyfriend – the father,
   carrying the basket.
There was no avoiding the fact
that he was a nice young kid.
   [If you will allow a digression here,
   as my father's DNA surfaces,
   as beautiful, and I guess traditional,
   as these baskets are; and I know
   newborns don't move that much;
   still with one handle and open,
   they look disturbingly unsafe.]

Its funny, on each of these three occasions,
after the initial uncontrollable response,
I went through the exact same routine.
First I would mutter "Bad luck."
   about running into her.
Followed by telling/reminding myself,
"Look she had no obligation to fall for you.
   Some strange old guy."
So I did make attempts to balance.

      When I speak of a strong (wordless) intuition
      I understand it as receiving a form of intelligence.
      The sense I got, long after the fact,
      was that God wanted this child.
      I don't mean this like a fundamentalist or Catholic,
         that God wants all.
      Of course that has a broad (and shallow) truth
      from the perspective of looking back
         at all of Creation as an accomplished whole.
      But that isn't what I'm trying to express.
      I mean very specifically this child.
      Not too surprising really.
      The girl's a wonderful girl, its to be expected
      that her daughter would be a wonderful child.
      Of course at the time I wasn't happy to discover
      that this had always been part of the plan
         (the baby as one of the 'two's.)
      But what was surprising to me in the intuition
      was the inference that God wanted the child
         but didn't want the girl to marry.
      My surmise, at the time - and afterwards actually,
      was that God knew if she married
      I would close the door forever, it would be final.
      For some reason it seemed God didn't want that.
      I thought what is more significant
         a piece of paper - or a baby?
      Don't get me wrong, I respect marriage a great deal,

but I think a baby is more significant.
I know I'm an ant, with only one window: my life.
What I've seen through that window,
in this instance what I witnessed in my sister's life,
after she fell for a likeable guy and they got married.
He was a Vietnam vet and in my opinion disturbed.
My sister never had any children with him.
Later, after converting to Islam, she remarried,
    and had her children.
To me there was something, maybe not conscious,
    that told her in the earlier relationship,
        this isn't right.
(Though I understand the range of people,
with lives and values extremely diverse,
    relative to specific circumstances,
so one shouldn't lay out any static rules.)

I wasn't so gaga on my divine destiny
that I wasn't aware that young people fall in love.
Or when they fall in love they often make love,
and often when they make love a baby results.
Nor is my position on abortion
    what you might expect from a leftist
(not that I lack discretion - I'm not a Jainist.)
Of course I am for keeping abortion a legal option,
    with medical support;
and leaving the decision up to the girl or woman.
But I respect the other side,
regard it as an issue where both sides are right:
    The fetus is not a baby.
    Yet if left alone it would be.
So I feel I'm respectful, not dismissive,
thinking only dumb religious atavists
could conflate embryos and fetuses with babies.
It's the same with the decision after birth,
    there is no right or wrong.
A young woman who decides she's not ready
does something hard but realistic

in giving the baby over to adoption.
Allowing those longing for a child their chance.
The young woman who decides to keep her baby
   does something brave and wonderful.
There is no wrong, they're both right.

So she broke free
and doesn't have to worry about me.
I'd do anything to avoid her.
Every time I would drive to that town
I'd pray God to at least grant me the mercy
   of not running into her again.
Isn't that pathetic?
Since I believe God wanted that child
I assume He'll protect her and the child.
Its her soul that will trouble her, nagging,
   'This isn't where we're supposed to be.
   This isn't the life we were supposed to lead.'
But I don't know how, as an answer,
you could beat: God wanted this child.
That sanctions everything she did.

        Not the 'surprise ending' I would have wanted
          though I know often the 'ideal' isn't ideal.

    If to conceive of God
       as your matchmaker
    is a spiritually dangerous conceit,
       what do you do
    when that is what you believe?

I just don't get it.
I don't understand the whole point of it all.
From any perspective.
If the ultimate goal was to have me
   end up with the girl,
with what was fated to occur
why have the prophecy at all?

Hopes sky-high, a 35 – 40 year build-up,
all walloped when it goes bust.
Why arrange the most extreme encounter,
    the pure being test,
if its only going to fail?
Now I associate her with the long torment,
and what's attractive about narrow and cold?
    a true love who doesn't chose true love.
On the other hand if it was all about punishment,
    a reckoning for my transgressions,
again it makes no sense to have someone so cold.
Better to have someone open and warm,
seriously considering, only at the end balking,
opting for an alternative closer in age.
    I was destroyed as it was,
but if it had had that personal more intimate turn,
    it would have hurt more
        than just God playing games on me.

Its all very well to command
forgiveness and trust,
    the assumption of a stepfather role,
but when the beloved has been frigid
a cause of hurt
love itself used as a tool against you…
    I must be missing something

                Its not her fault
                God deliberately picked someone too young.
                Its God's fault.

Wouldn't you agree that expectation,
to a very large extent, keys response?
If you're looking for salvation and blissful love,
and you get crushed, you have one result.
Take the exact same circumstances though
    with no expectations
        and they unfold harmlessly

    beautiful local girl moved away
    got pregnant   had a baby   life

Gurdjieff, an esoteric master,
believed individuals (and societies)
periodically needed 'shocks'.
So maybe all this was a shock
to prod me to finish these books.

It struck me as perverse
that when all hope was extinguished
it should be raised from the ashes
    only to be slain again.
Excuse me for slighting the gift of renewed life,
but what if the prophecy's purpose,
besides nudging you away from wrong choices,
    and towards the right one,
was to swell hope back up, revive you,
lead you not to suspect the hit coming,
all so that blow would be staggering?
It wasn't about delivering,
the object was to keep you in the game
and string it out as far as it could stretch.

II. Thoughts

I want to reiterate how an account like this,
compressing a good portion of a life,
    can't help but distort.
It doesn't convey how uncertainty
permeated all assessments and decisions.
I wasn't constantly receiving secret messages,
    or witnessing supernatural stunts.
My routine was as mundane and boring as yours
    (if yours is exciting I apologize.)
Occasionally some disturbing powers were in play.
Events occurred that weren't normal or natural,
    but these were rare.
Some edicts you had to keep in mind.
But there is a human ability
to cover over troubling thoughts
    attention absorbed
in the occupations and busyness of the day.

I have an eccentric mindset
    which I presume I was built with.
As a child I zealously subscribed
to all of my parents beliefs
and they were (very moral) atheists,
who advocated casting aside old 'superstitions',
religion as 'opiate of the masses'
fabricated to manipulate the credulous
for the benefit of the ruling few.
My parents viewed the world as 100% material.
The spiritual was all fantasy.
As a child their views were mine.
Yet even with my allegiance to what they held
I could never fully embrace
the 'we are free if we decide to be' ethic.
I couldn't put it into words of course
    - or even thoughts -
but what I felt was the opposite:

we were all contained,
we moved inside an already determined play.
People could kid themselves,
   especially when muscling an activity,
   which yields a sense of accomplishment,
but it was all an illusion - a necessary illusion.
Independence and freedom
   were ultimately self-deceptions.
Considering my conformity to my parents views,
   as far from Predestination as you could get,
this was an odd intuition for an obedient child.
When I look at such a person getting cast
I vacillate between two extremes.
   The oddness of a lost daydreaming type
   raised on the political and material.
   It seems to make no sense,
   I shake my head and wonder if it can be true.
   Oppositely I sometimes think,
      No, a background of absolutely blankness
      is a perfect proof and qualification,
         as its free of bias.

The fact that I'm the type people would doubt
simply adds to the perfection of the selection.

                When I consider if a niece
                told me she'd fallen
                for someone 40 years older
                my initial response
                would not be a happy one.
                Before I could accept
                I would need to be convinced
                   her love was deep,
                strong enough to endure his aging,
                that he was a good soul
                   and his love for her
                went beyond her young body,
                to the person she was.

Though I knew, even during the worst moments,
that you don't have a right to require another
to follow your secret script;
it was something I knew – but not what I felt.
In my mind she had come to be part of it all,
so when it turned out to be a setup
she represented – was the embodiment
   of the hurt and what I took to be fraudulence.
Plus I have a psychological bent
   whenever there's a setback blow
   or I find myself marooned in awfulness
I search for a suitable scapegoat.
As if finding one will solve the problem,
I'll offload the bad, and be freed somehow.

The fact that the attraction wasn't as strong
as it was supposed to be,
had to be, to get the match to work,
to overcome the uncertainties on both sides,
   couldn't be anyone's fault.
The girl couldn't have been more innocent,
a victim of a fate she didn't have a clue about.
God was intent on tricking me.
She was used – held up as the reward.
(She really was **the one**
   so the test would count.)
Too young.
Strange as it was for me, after so many years
to finally enter the long rumored space,
and find nothing proceeding as I had supposed,
it must have been stranger for her,
everything a perplexity,
no touchstones to get her bearings by.
Unknown play, characters, actors.
Coming from a conservative background,
   trained to be judgmental,
not old enough to trust herself.

>   And not to forget that we shouldn't scant
>   that a person feels what they feel.
>   If they have mixed emotions
>   they have mixed emotions.

>   The paradox of a girl
>   who disobeyed her soul,
>   and thereby fulfilled God's will,
>   is beyond me to comprehend,
>   let alone reconcile.

When you're young, impatient,
you have an unquenchable thirst for answers.
Later you become more accepting (and wary).
Though the mystical states were fairly constant,
the psychic & supernatural were rare
and as I said normally occurred
    only when I was sober.
If the prophecy was an exception – then granted,
though I don't think I could have been that stoned.
But there were exceptions,
and the most frequent ones were
    when I got really high on LSD.
With no warning the Absolute
would interrupt the proceedings
    with some inexplicable communiqué.
One I never figured out:

> *halcyon days of yore*
> *- yore is like some place you've been before.*

[along with:] *How dead do you want to be?*
               Well you write the book in our history.

This was typical of their nature and tone,
an enigmatic correction from a severe teacher.
At first you feel a reverential wow
    (not that you miss the gibe

    that you'd never had any 'halcyon days'),
an encounter with the Absolute
never gets old, and can't help but produce awe.
I don't know if the expression 'wrote the book'
    (for establishing the record) is still extant;
and I should probably volunteer my take
    - shared by many others -
that the LSD trip was like dying.
Both the spiritually transcendent experience,
   but also the hard grim endurance.
   [And marijuana made me paranoid
     - so go figure.]
Its when you tried to decode the message
that you ended up frustrated and blurred.
'Halcyon days' was a phrase I never used.
Of course you hear and read these things,
but 'halcyon' was not in my vocabulary.
Instead of helping on that though
the amplification went to 'yore',
which, even if archaic, is a word
   pretty commonly understood.
You then stumble around with Greek legends:
calm seas for 14 days around winter solstice,
   mythological floating kingfisher nests…
You end up going around and around
   chasing your own tail.
These fixations never ended in a resolution.
Intellectual knotting, entropy, airless tedium.
Our fundamentalist friends might say,
   'Aha this proves it's a familiar spirit!'
No, it was all God.
And I don't doubt it had a heavy meaning.
I'm sure it did, and one day it'll fall on my head.
But you are forced to give up
not waste any more time trying to unscramble
something intentionally made so impermeable.
   How does a mythical kingfisher
   relate to anything in our reality?

Anyway these things aren't helpful -
they manifest as landmark confirmations
only after whatever is referred to has occurred.

    To have hope prolongs pain.
    I outgrew ambitions in rock,
    maybe I matured beyond marriage
        and the energy required,
    held onto it as an old fantasy fixation,
    without doing the preparatory work.
    Yet if she hadn't turned out so cold –
    if she had approached, opened, chosen me,
    I think it could have been
        fulfillment   happiness   arrival
    celebratory joy overflowing, seeming unreal
        only because it was so expansive.

            I want to ask your indulgence – go with me
            on yet another difficult circuitous concept.
            This one: the Absolute's ability
            to fit a sentence to match a person's
                reaction to that sentence.
            I know.
            Remember to Providence the future
            is as concrete as the past.
            It knows not only what will happen,
            but how you will react.
            I speak as one who believes
                he's witnessed this looping.
            Anyway I'm obliged to bring this up
            in case my test/punishment fate
            followed this route, which I think likely.
                A subject judged unworthy
                because he couldn't forgive.
            Thought experiment:
            Focus on my disgraceful response
            cut off from what precipitated it.
            Assaying the behavior on its own.

        Now think of a 'test' - and a sentence -
        designed to punish that faulty response.
        That's what happened. (I think.
        I won't deny this fits my metaphysics,
        but I'd argue I have these metaphysics
        because of the life I had.)
        Even if I had been right
            about a 'pure being test'
        what I missed
        was that there never was a chance
            that we could pass.

On acting like a responsible human being
I was laggard, but eventually came around.
If you were out in the woods
    when I was cutting a tree
it was wise to get as far away as you could.
I had no idea which way the tree would fall,
my guess seemed wrong more often than right.
I couldn't tell you how many times a tree
would rock back and bind the chainsaw blade.
Then I'd whack away with my axe,
drive wedges in with my doublejack
   - and they'd get stuck in their turn.
I'd spend over an hour on this frantic labor
and the tree would still fall wrong way back.
Later I gave the whole business up
- though I loved going into the woods.
I had saved money so I could finally buy
    a new first class chainsaw.
It turned out to be the only lemon
I'd ever heard of that company producing.
I figured the Absolute's message was: stop
its dangerous and you're no good at it.

The tree in the incident was an old monster.
Dead for a good while
but at ground level the wood wasn't punky.

My saw was good size, but not for this tree,
I had to walk in a circle to complete the cut.
But when I did I wondered
    'why are you still standing?'
I was able to yank the chainsaw out,
held it in one hand
and did one of those irrational acts
you do when you're tired and frustrated,
I pushed with my other arm on the trunk
    though my sensible self knew that
with the weight of this great tree
there was no way a tiny human could budge it.
But, just then, it started to go - that crack sound.
I stared in disbelief.
Usually when I'd lapse into one of my staring
    is-Existence-going-to-free-me? trances
there wouldn't be anyone around;
    or at least not anyone who knew me.
But that day my brother-in-law was there,
and he was yelling at me to run.
As I said these reactions weren't conscious,
    - and yet they weren't unconscious either
(maybe there's a small middle state in between,
and their tension makes paralysis easier).
It was the biggest widow-maker I'd ever seen.
A widow-maker, as I understand it
    is the dead top of a tree
    which can fall when the tree is cut
    or more often, as in this case,
breaking when it hits a green tree
then getting launched back.
A man who had worked briefly with loggers
told me this story he heard about a logging crew.
A certain guy, kind of a sidekick character,
    jumped on top of a tree as soon as it landed.
    There was a delay before the widow-maker
        came down and killed him.
    The crew simply put his body to the side

and finished the day's work. He was dead.
This flying spear was so massive, so impressive,
it could have slain a Titan.
   [Wait – error. Titans were immortal,
     that's why they were imprisoned in Tartarus.]
It was coming right at me, which made sense,
getting slung back in the direction
   from which it came.
But then another one of those occurrences:
as it was flying forward, perfectly horizontal,
   it snapped in two.
Both pieces then rotated to perfect verticals,
with their heavier bottoms leading them down.
I never moved an inch.
The massive piece shook the ground when it hit.
The tip was lighter and the height of a man.
It landed near me and fell forward,
pushing me in the shoulder without hurting me,
as in the manner of a friend saying,
   "Wake up!"
That was it. I finally took stock of my behavior.
I like to think of myself as a moral being.
I thought
   If the Absolute is going to expend energy
   to keep a worthless worm alive,
   the least the worthless worm can do
   is to make an effort to act responsibly.

                I have no grounds on which to reproach her.
                You can't say someone was cold for 5 years,
                and then turn around and say they misled you.

        I should make it clear
        that I had no permission to concoct
        my fairy tale elaborations.
        You're not supposed to make things up,
        adding whatever you like.
        Now a lot of it not only appears wrong,

poorly supported, but childishly self-serving.
The entrant staggering across the finish line
   proclaimed: the winner! -
to be rewarded with love and recognition.

The prophecy was a marvel,
   puzzling and dense,
   packed with various meanings
   going in multiple directions.
But its brevity left great gaps
   and I had so many years.
I thought I was being careful,
heedful of what had been given
   - simply filling in.
I presumed the promise
   was blissful happiness,
so the true love would look at me
I'd look at her
   We'd know
Doubts dispelled forever
Love quickly followed by artistic success.
It never occurred to me
   ('in deep' notwithstanding)
that the culmination could be
   mystery compounded.

      All those years I assumed the love
         would be magical,
      have some special power,
         not something a person could veto.
      I hadn't foreseen the pure being test,
      but it wouldn't have mattered if I had.
      After all it was going to be a woman
         anointed by God,
      the match a perfect one.
      I always assumed - if it did happen –
         it would be incredibly unique.
      This isn't to say anything against God's girl.

She's wonderful, and shouldn't be penalized
for being sensible, or having her own taste;
opting for someone familiar and known,
over some old guy who looked at her funny.
What I mean is I assumed the force/power
  would be so strong. Nuclear.
  that nothing could knock it awry.

    Now a different metaphor suggests itself.
    God has His own collider.
    Two are shot at the speed of light
    accelerated in opposite directions
      aimed at each other
      so when they smash
    everything inside can be traced.

        If the point is to establish
        that the love I mustered
        was not unconditional,
        I have no defense.
        As long as its conceded
        that it was blind faith love
        for a stranger
        who was too young
          cold
            conservative
        and the 'condition' was a baby.
        Then yes, I admit
        it was not unconditional love.

    Why not someone warm?

Its my fault
I couldn't adapt.
Maybe after so many years I got rigid.
When things didn't go as I expected
I was inflexible, unable to adjust.
A true love that was too young

      to even speak to
      was a blow that stunned.
When she turned enigmatic and cold
      it knocked me sideways.
A baby by another -
      I was knocked out.

I never had a backup plan.
I thought to even contemplate such a thing
would demonstrate lack of faith.
It never occurred to me anyway that
if the foretold started clicking into place
   that it wouldn't all work out.
I accepted that the prophecy could evaporate,
   turn out to be an illusion;
but not that if it started coming true
   anything but good could follow good.

There were a few wrinkles I took well.
That she came from conservatives,
   might not be too intellectual or literary.
If the Absolute wanted a cosmic alliance,
I could understand and go with this variance
even though I had assumed a soulmate
would be someone on my wave-length,
   even a partisan for my writing.
One thing I had learned in the long interval
was that the intellectual was a narrow sphere.
Many who had no regard for it,
   who lived without it, and saw it as artificial,
were balanced people living very full lives.
Not having that extra reflection
   didn't seem to diminish them in the least.
Maybe it was a non-essential sensitivity.
So I wouldn't say I flunked on everything.
On the other hand I'm sure a superior man
confronting the same circumstances
could have mustered more understanding,

been less emotional, broader, more 'mature'.
Nine out of ten of them would have reacted:
   'She's wonderful – so young.
      With a little baby girl?
      That's no problem.'
So I'm the embittered one out of ten going:
   'I didn't wait 40 years for this.
   To be a white bread's second choice
      - if I'm lucky.
   God can keep his girl.'
Unfortunately that was my reaction.
What can I do about it though?
People are different.
You pretty much are who you are.

I did realize it was lunacy to be mad at a girl
for not following a script she knew nothing about.
So I had a bright idea
   inspired by 'no-fault' divorce
to ask God why not a no-fault dissolution,
a spiritual annulment?
   In light of developments
   the prophecy was no longer relevant.
Why not declare it no longer binding?
   With no fault assessed onto either party.
She's not to blame for reasonable doubts;
   resisting what didn't feel strong enough,
   not resisting what did.
Since God had pointed her out to me,
with what I took to be a promise
   of blissful happiness,
and instead it turned out to be a botch,
I should be let off the hook as well.
Why not release both parties from the contract?
If she isn't allowed
to find someone 40 years older dubious,
   then Judgment lacks fairness.
If I'm not allowed to say 'No I don't accept',

after waiting 40 years, and getting passed over,
    then Judgment lacks understanding.
The stillness that greeted this great idea
    was of a particular tenor.
Not that of a message misaddressed – lost,
no reply because the query never arrived.
It was more a deliberate ignoring notice
reserved for fools who lacked the wit
to catch on that everything
    - including all the items of their squawking -
had been covered in the original exposition.

        If I'm right about the dynamic
            I don't envy the girl
        that split with her soul.
        I have a good imagination
        but I can't fully imagine that.
        With all my conflicts at least that's one
            I'm not aware of suffering.
        Now if we were talking about conscience
        I'd be obliged to step forward and *testify*.

        Yet I've always been one with my soul.
        It had to partake of all of my black moods
            depressions   despairs   feelings of failure.
        While I was able to rely on its belief.
        As I've said
        I thought God was more or less stuck with me,
            though I did worry that I could blow it.
        But I never considered
        (difficult as her blind path must have been)
        that an anointed could turn out wobbly.
        Since she had to possess a rare spiritual purity
        I never imagined that such a person
            could have a rift with her soul,
        let alone that the soul could lose to the mind.
        In hindsight I should have considered that
            since she had no firm knowledge of me,

with youth's repugnance towards age,
not knowing which impulses to trust,
gossip: 'he's unattached, probably gay',
and coming from the reactionary camp
with all its pigeonholes and prejudices,
taking a pass on me was extremely rational.

My childishly simplistic conceptions
I must admit I got what I deserved.
I must turn in the required work(s).
Suppress my grumbling. Even mentally.

> God has taught me a lot
> I just don't know it

You can't tell God what's what.
The Absolute's position seemed to be
   You can't reject her
   anymore than she can reject you.
   She can't succeed or fail
   anymore than you can succeed or fail.
   Or do you still imagine you've graduated?
Her perception, without any knowledge
or any psychic aid, must have been difficult.
Then factor in God wanting that child.
Though I couldn't see it at the time
I bet we both swerved as far as we could.
As I've come to understand the relationship
   I believe the behavior will balance.
The errors may differ in kind,
but in the end they will be equal.
They must add up to the exact same amount.

I may never have been worthy,
having fallen too far before it all began.
Add being unforgiving and mistrustful.
Swearing I'd never raise another's child,
a provocation - setting a precondition.

If you're unworthy you can wait forever
    it won't make you a tragic figure.

Though I couldn't tell you
how, from where, I derived the idea
that true love wouldn't (couldn't)
    pick the wrong person,
that is what I believed.
So when another fathered her child
in my mind she had gone too far,
she had failed the test.
I think that's how the notion
    of the *forbidden* came into it.

                    I'm _____ed, and probably for keeps.
                      I don't believe in reincarnation.
                      If I did I could say well maybe next life
                          things might work out.
                      We could find ourselves closer in age,
                          having learned our lessons.
                      Or switching: the right person for each
                          would be someone else.
                      But I believe in one life - then eternity.
                          So that's it.
                      And I don't believe God makes mistakes.
                      The girl didn't cooperate with my scheme
                      but it wasn't an accident.
                      From this point on
                      I shouldn't deceive myself,
                      and more importantly
                      I shouldn't deceive anyone else.
                      I may have trouble with the reality result,
                      too bad, it doesn't change what stands.

    Aren't there male animals who will turn away
    from any female who already has an offspring?

                      You can't get outside the game.

Here I want to tell you about a Bible story
    that always bothered me.
Jacob agrees to work for Laban for 7 years
    in order to receive Rachel as his wife.
When the 7 years are up Laban tricks him.
At night, after the wedding feast, he slips Leah into
Jacob's bed - which makes her his wife.
Laban explains that its the custom in this country
    that the older sister marries first.
Jacob gets Rachel but only for an additional 7 years.
I always found this story so oppressive -
    how was all this tolerable - permissible?
This rank duplicity under the supervision of God.
This is how the 12 tribes come about?
And the preceding Rebecca/Isaac story was similar,
    full of premeditated machinations.
Rebecca overhears old blind Isaac instructing Esau,
his favorite, to hunt and prepare some savory venison
so as to inspire a most favorable final blessing.
She prepares a fake version of this stew
and guides Jacob (her favorite), to pass for his brother,
to steal the blessing of good fortune and superiority.
Jacob lies to his father and the trickery works.
I knew these were origin stories of primitive people
    but still it was all too crude and burdensome.
Even when Laban and Jacob finally agree to part ways,
Laban is scheming to cheat and Jacob is busy outwitting.
Most of Jacob's children reveal some character flaw
which, like a curse, shapes the fate of their descendants.
Yet what strikes me as odd, and I only see it now,
is that the wrong me was reading these accounts,
    completely out of chronological order.
It should have been the 'rational' skeptical child,
raised by atheists, dismissive of all things supernatural.
But it wasn't. It was the frame of a much later mind,
the one that believed in the primacy of the spiritual,
    and saw a plasticity to the phenomenal world.

Who saw a relativity and evolution to matter's solidity;
earlier times and places were subject to different rules,
    dependent on what their people believed.
In time laws coalesced, objects became more concrete,
hardening and conforming to a modern 'universal' reality.
To say our world is more 'real' than our ancestors
obscures the fact that together we created this world,
via consensus consciousness. Agreeing and confirming.
It was anachronistic for my younger self to accept
the stories of Moses, the prophecies of the prophets,
Jesus's miracles, healings, and casting out of demons.
    (As well as last blessings possessing power.)
And that younger self shouldn't have cared about
what behavior a purported bronze age deity allowed.
(Yet it wasn't my ultimate maturer understanding,
which came to see more clearly, in a deeper way,
the human participation in the Whole or Absolute.)

As things turned out I'm sorry
the girl and I ever encountered each other.
I regret having whatever effect I had on her.
Who wants to be a disruptive influence
    in a young girl's life? Not me.
It never occurred to me as a possibility
that events could unfold the way they did.
True love used like a decoy. (If it was.)

Though I still like the 2 lines.
Still believe they were inspired.

        If I could firmly unequivocally state
        that there's no blame to be laid on the girl...
        Certainly she had no way to know
        of a prophecy I carried in my head,
        or expectations built over a 35-40 year wait.
        The problem is, for some reason
        I can only go partway towards that assessment.
        Not all the way.

What I can swear to as true
is that if someone had come to me beforehand
and laid out every detail of what was to transpire,
with the calmest confidence I would have replied,
'No, that's impossible. That could never happen.'
Even now it all seems unreal.
If over these years the only recourse God had
to keep me alive (and awake) was mental torture,
   this might reveal a personal weakness,
     or a general human susceptibility. Or both.

               The pitch was always going to be:
               can't you see how young she is?
               Too young to know.
               Where is your heart?
               While poor form I can't help knowing
               that everything's at God's discretion.
               It'll get added to my deficiency of gratitude,
               to look there, and not at her youth as a gift.
               Lack of compassion, tolerance, scope.
                   Why can't I accept
               a little misstep here or there?

                      It's a wonderful test
                      if no answer is the right answer

   If you had been told the truth
   You wouldn't have continued

III. just living

Here's an anecdote - a humorous break
   from Eric's dark tale of undeserved woe.
I take care of my mother during the warm months,
she stays with my sister for the cold.
The transition usually occurs around Thanksgiving.
My sister and her husband, their five grown kids,
   could not be more loving and gracious,
but you have to understand that for Muslims
not all of our big holidays are free from friction.
Thanksgiving however, centered around the family,
   with the ideal of thankfulness,
can be joined in without reservation.
My wonderful Sister is a great cook,
   with her eldest son and daughter helping,
     usually with many non-family guests invited
     its always a giant celebratory feast.
So the morning after, happy, feeling full,
I walk to the marina, wearing my SF Giant's sweatshirt.
It's a beautiful, invigoratingly cool morning.
Setting (for me) a brisk pace, feeling healthy,
on my return walk back a woman in a car,
young daughter in the backseat, pulls over to the curb.
I assume she's about to ask where some street is.
My Father had absolutely no directional sense,
which I've inherited. I could get lost anywhere.
And the Bay area is so complex – forget it.
I've prepared my 'I'm sorry, I'm a tourist' response
but she asks, "Are you hungry?"
I'm thrown. "No, I had a big dinner yesterday."
She's very nice, gives me a "God Bless" salutation.
Back at the house my story draws yucks.
I'm obviously fazed, which amuses everyone more.
   "Yes you ate yesterday. But what about today?"
I'm really not that far removed from the poorest,
but getting mistaken for a homeless person,
coming so unexpectedly, was disorienting.

Anyway you can understand, given this incident,
that when I returned to the mountains,
and later shaved for the first time in decades,
my Mother might see this incident
as the proximate cause, or prod, for the change.
    (For a writer it's a good lesson
      of the powerless dilemma of being captured
        as a character in another's story.)
But I can assure you there was little connection.

I knew a couple, and was very fond of both.
    They had one child, a little boy.
They were spiritual in the same way I am.
If you want to call it New Age that's fine by me.
I could only remember my friend with a beard.
They moved back east for a bit, and he shaved.
    I don't know why - or if that matters.
The important thing was the effect it had on her.
She described it as a trauma.
    Who is this person I'm married to?
This made such an impression on me.
I had never considered facial hair important.
It was external. Like clothes or your car. Appearance.
But because I respected her so much,
    as a spiritual being, it made a deep impression.
I vowed if the prophecy ever did come true
before the marriage took place I would shave,
so the girl/woman could see what she was getting,
    and if she freaked out,
she'd have time to call off the wedding.
Trust me I never forgot that commitment,
    if the girl had fallen for me
      I was primed to follow through.
So that was why the idea was in my mind.
When everything collapsed and I was on my own,
    feeling dissatisfied – seeing myself as boring,
I thought why not shave anyway,

  shake things up, do something different?
It didn't change anything.
Except when I'm walking and wave at a car
the people inside wonder
'who is that fellow waving at us?'

    In the end if I read the signs right
    and my late assessments were correct,
    then a lot of what I had assumed
     (obviously) was wrong.
    That true love will always chose true love.
    That true love can't pick the wrong person
     (if the right person is present).
    I couldn't tell you
    where I derived these concepts,
     let alone all the adjuncts
      I tagged on.

    As I said, if you had posed the hypothetical
    of true loves circling each other
     but the magnetic attraction
    proving not strong enough to unite,
    I would have said, 'No – that's not possible.
    That's a contradiction of the very definition.'
    If you went further and specified this pairing
     was one ordained by God,
    that would have made my rejection
    even more emphatic, more unconditional:
     'You've gotten something wrong.
     Think what you're saying! It's impossible.'
    Another thing I misunderstood,
    with my perfect match & balance template
     (after I'd fallen in love with her)
    was that the slippage and mismatching
     could be sequential.
    I have the prophecy. I fall for her.
    She's in the dark. Demurs and rejects.
    I react to that.

If she changes her mind, its too late for me.
Now I'm the one who negates.
Its still match & balance perfection,
only – fittingly - not together in time,
    but staggered.
Which actually makes it even more perfect,
with the negatives balancing the positives.

  The boundary was found
    but once passed…

        The Absolute needed lost-in-mystery
        I suppose to shuffle irreconcilables,
        an intended child fathered by another
          with an idealized couple.

I think you hurt more when you're young
Unprepared   You don't know what to expect
There's more of you then   You feel more
Your enthusiasm pushes past warnings.
When you're older there's not only less of you,
but the naïve faith and openness is gone.
    You're worn and wary,
the scarred hide harder and thicker.
So I can't say this ordeal hurt most,
but I can say it was the biggest disappointment.
I'd buried hope for the most part
yet when, right after my father's death,
the prophecy started activating
there was a knocking on the casket wall,
a quickening – eyes looking for light and life.
    Re-encasing the heart has been harder
        and taken longer
            than expected.

After the cave-in of the promise occurred
it also caused a conflicting bewilderment
    about how to set my bearings.

After so many years of stasis,
when in every critical transit before
the Absolute had intervened to save me,
I was now trapped in a fate set-up,
engineered by that same Providence.
How could I have anticipated that?

One answer might be
that if I hadn't been so dedicated
to forcing a happy ending interpretation
I might have picked up on the truer meanings
   of 'freeze'
    and 'in deep'
and that could have clued me to the possibility
that fate and flesh might turn against me
becoming alien, cold, even hostile.

                I assumed it was faith and endurance.
                That was the focus, and should I pass
                all would be revealed. To my benefit.
                But when it turned out the 40 years
                were preliminary to the real test
                    (of all my weaknesses)
                I crumpled into recrimination and self-pity.

                You know in American Indian belief
                  - where 'medicine' means more –
                they say your remedy
                will exist near the problem.
                (Is that a 'faith in Creation'?)

                My feeling – or complaint,
                that these trials had no purpose,
                    aside from torment,
                is hard to maintain
                if we look at this long poem
                as an attempt to record
                    what I learned.

        I have no more volition than a cork
           floating on top of the ocean
        with no idea where the tides will take me
          with no ability to move on my own

          If I make it now I'll barely make it.

You had two individuals
unable to penetrate the surface of the other,
unable to perceive what lay within.

It won't surprise you
that a conservative not choosing real love
fits – flows right into my biases.
But I think it will surprise you
that I held the fact that
she went through the pregnancy by herself,
locking me out of that experience,
as a separate unforgiveable offense.
It makes no sense. The child wasn't mine,
presumably the biological father was there.
I know emotions are often illogical
but this is bizarrely perverse:
    Having the baby is unforgiveable.
    Not sharing the experience is unforgiveable.
Yet I feel there is something underneath this.
It may go back to the conception
of how a soulmate is supposed to behave.

             I believe its true
             humility is needed
             to clear a space
             to allow the spiritual to come in.

             Maybe I've understood humility as a good
                too intellectually
             not sufficiently relaxing the asserting self.

> How arrogant will it seem
> if I say she passed God's test,
>   did what God wanted,
> but didn't pass my test?
> God is all of Creation.

I was staggering before the surprise trick ending,
even before 2006. (If I need to admit that.)
Its funny when it looks like its all over
and there's this feeling that you've gone beyond -
    there isn't much of you left,
maybe you've learned things along the way
    but bits were torn off.
I had this conception
- from a W.C. Fields movie I'd seen:
for some exigent dramatic reason Fields needs
to keep his steamboat going at top speed.
To do this he tears off parts of the boat
and keeps throwing them into the boiler.
I felt like that was what I was doing,
only I wasn't just the person, I was also the boat.
Then sometime after 2006 this idiotic refrain:
    'no one likes me' or 'nobody likes me'
    (later it morphed into 'no one loves me')
kept intruding - coming into my mind,
and I couldn't stop it.
I know its origin, a kid's camp song:
    'Nobody likes me, everybody hates me.
       Guess I'll eat some worms…'
going on to describe various types of worms.
Wholly adolescent from beginning to end.
However for me to be unable to stop it,
    unable to block it,
there's no other way to assess this
except as a demented crack.

                    God has toyed with me

> To the true love
> I was some kind of curiosity
> she was never quite sure of

I won't be offended if you decide
that all I've described
are creations of my subconscious,
fantasies I've projected out,
tricking myself into taking
them as parts of the outer world
when in truth they come from within.
The way I view the world
all of it flowing into
   the Absolute Whole
which orchestrates the show,
our primary connection
is through the subconscious
   half discovering   half creating.
So its possible that while you think
   you're reducing my testimony
we're actually pretty close.

> The judgment was fair.
> A person who wants
>   a wife
>   and children
> should be committed to life,
> and I never was.

> When you no longer want to pass the test
> its hard to see God's angle.

> As I've told you
> I assumed if the prophecy came true
> it would signify that I had passed,
>   the price had been paid,
> from that point forward all would be free:

        Success, the perfect love
          - one stamped with God's seal.
     Yet, though she was the true love,
     there was no magical magnetic attraction.
     Instead: age gap, doubts, misunderstandings,
        everything out of whack.
     God's twist was to deliver the right person
       but have her present without any comprehension.
(The strange sense, as things fell away,
    confirming she was the one
    by your reaction to her defection.)
The destined child comes into being.
    The girl punished.
    I'm punished.
a beautiful knot
There was perfection in the play,
not as I envisioned, a fairytale denouement,
but a train-wreck full of Justice.
The impurities in my conduct and attitude
    had not gone unobserved.
I don't know what the girl did wrong
but I could never argue my presumptuousness
didn't warrant a devastating correction.
Engineered in an amazingly ingenious manner
(I was thinking how 'brilliant' it was
    when I caught myself,
of course it was brilliant – it was God.)

I had been trying to console myself
   'Alright, maybe no wife, no children,
  but you will be free in the next world.'
This wasn't made up succor,
its based on what I believe,
that there is a fundamental balance
   considering a person's circumstances
  when they pass into the eternal.
A built-in compensation
   for every deprivation.

Think appreciations and freedoms.
No loss without a gain in other words.
Go ahead raise your eyebrows
   and roll your eyes
      but that is what I believe.
Not simply because to exist is a blessing,
   and to regret what happened
is the same as regretting your existence
   (though I believe that too.)
I'm emphasizing here an elemental balance
taken into account before Creation
   and in Creation
factoring what would be given
and what would not be given.

It was only when I dwelt on how my hope
had ended up in a mortuary
(in our county the surname of the father
has been associated with funeral homes,
   so I figured a probable 'connection'),
not the quick death & rebirth I expected,
   more like getting buried alive
   drawn out indefinite limbo
that I remembered lines from long ago:

      Trichinosis soul
      and I'm so free.
      Free to walk
      in the Obsidian Building

All these years later I'm not sure
if it was 'walk' or 'wander',
but I don't think that affects the meaning.
And 'building' was stretched out: build-ding,
(I don't know why or what it indicates.)
I was going to tell you when this occurred,
   but I don't really remember
and you shouldn't trust my memory anyway.

Let's leave it as a long time ago.
What I did know from the first
    was that the person speaking was me.
Not just because of the "I'm",
but because the sardonic laconic
    was (is) one of my primary modes.
I didn't know what time it referred to,
    if it applied to the present or the future.
I thought it might be framing a mood.
A soul sickened by what it had imbibed.
You have to break down 'trichinosis',
    sound out 'trick', and 'gnosis'
        which is secret spiritual knowledge.
And you need to know the association
of obsidian with human sacrifice.
Confinement in a temple tomb.

There are two backstories I need to relate.
One is from family history.
Though she became completely secular
my mother's family was (Reform) Jewish.
Having rational convictions, she tried to give
rational explanations for religious rules.
Her absolute favorite example
was the prohibition against eating pig.
She explained pork could go bad
in the days before refrigeration,
and people would get seriously ill.
So the leaders decided to tell the people
that God forbade them to eat pigs.
They obeyed this as a Divine decree.
The offshoot: while other people got sick,
    the Jews didn't.

The second tie-in was more recent.
One day, as a conversation starter,
lamely trying to get anything rolling,
with a weather system coming in,

I commented on that prospect to the girl.
She, chilly, wasn't pleased, commenting
that later on she had to catch piglets,
   i.e. hard enough in good conditions.
My response was odd and inexplicable,
I stammered, "I didn't understand".
I usually do pretty well on my feet,
   but this was weirdly incongruent.
What didn't I understand? Chasing piglets?
Of course with everything going screwy
   why not stutter-mutter nonsense.

Now that I recalled the trichinosis lines
I knew this was the time they applied to.
I always assumed the prophecy stood alone.
Usually these bits are discrete to themselves.
So I presumed the trichinosis lines
   were independent of anything else.
     I no longer believe that to be the case.
     I had been tricked by secret knowledge.
     I was buried alive.
     And there was a human sacrificial element.
     The worst part was its direct aim mocking
     of how I was trying to console myself,
       that I'd be free in heaven.
     I was hooked, and I'd stay hooked.
     I was captive, and I'd stay captive.
     It struck me as very Old Testamentish:
       You will accept everything.
       It is not for you to decline.

                    I must say - unless I'm crazy
                    my life's been unusual
                    (if I'm crazy – not unusual)

              I don't mind eating confusion
                 if I have no choice,
              but that's not what I wanted to produce,

>   or pass on to readers.
>   That's not why I became a writer.

>   fitting for a prophecy
>   that came true
>   while not coming true.
>   I 'learn my lesson' -
>   and don't learn my lesson.

>   There's nothing wrong
>   while you're young and beautiful
>   with falling in love
>   with a young man intoxicated
>   by your beauty and grace.
>   One of the great crests in life -
>   emotional swell and surge
>   moving inspired – enchanted,
>   high, filled with a giving spirit.
>   Begrudge the girl this experience?
>   I don't think I do.

It seems, partial as I am,
that the judgment-punishment
was more appropriate for someone
who thought he was smarter than God.
I have a lot of faults,
but I don't think that is one of them.
Sometimes I think I'm smarter than everyone else
    but that doesn't include God.
I've shared with you my conception of God.
I wonder if it could be disobedience either,
    when commanded I'm a total dog.
Maybe not happy about my condition
(even dogs get to feel what they feel.)
The real rift occurred with the birth,
which I'd argue was a case of knowing myself:
This is something I won't be able to overcome.
Presumably God's contention was: Yes you will.

Well?
Can knowing your own limitations
be construed as obstinacy or rebellion?

> The perfect punishment
> for someone unable to forgive
> is to arrange circumstances
> so he can't forgive his true love.
> I can see and concede that.
> Still nothing will stop me from adding
> that the rigged setup was cruel.

In the years right after the prophecy [1968]
I did behave in a supremely arrogant manner.
Hubristic. If that was unforgivable I'm sunk.
But I was young, stoned and overwhelmed.
I thought I could mold - shape my fate.
My rationalization (this will make you laugh)
was Jesus. To be exact Matthew's Jesus,
who was always going around
deliberately arranging things
to bring some ancient prophecy to pass.
I thought if Jesus can stage events
for something as important
   as actualizing the Messiah,
I ought to have the flexibility to bend things
to make a personal prophecy work out
   the way I want it to.
Of course Matthew couldn't get a
Scriptural citation correct to save his life.
But I don't think that undercuts the testament,
its not scholarship, its simple observation.
An approach witnessed by all the disciples.
Matthew could have been misinformed,
yet this would be a very odd thing to invent.
What's the motive, for Matthew or anyone else?
Though I was in my 20's, looking back now,
it has about it an air of youthful impetuosity.

    (While rigidly unforgiving of others,
    I have a wonderful spirit of charity and kindness
       in understanding my own lapses.)

    It wasn't a blessing
    it was what it was.

I can't complain 'I want my just deserts!'
- my just deserts would be a firing squad.
Nor can I act like all the times God saved me
shouldn't be weighed in the judgment.
If ever anyone's life did not belong to them
   it would be mine.
It was two full years before I decompressed,
   the anger subsiding, spent,
and finally returned to my body and reality.
Settling into, regaining, a more grounded sanity.
I saw myself as I was. Old and poor.
I was able to start the reassessing and reasoning
   that if this was the sentence I deserved,
   her life, maybe even the shape of her soul
   could have been molded to accommodate.
How could I justify my inexcusable response?
It was okay that she had chosen someone else.
And I understood part of being 'wrung'
   had an artistic purpose,
   and a lodging in time.
I've tried to gather myself enough
to stand, learn, and slog on.
I was going to say that the Absolute
   had its little joke:
      Not Time
      Not Time
      Too Late.
   A true love who was perfect
except she didn't have true love.
   I get to be a creep
   without getting the girl.

But why not shed self-pity?
Admit it was a hard lesson,
admit, that with me, hard is the only way
anything ever penetrates - and sticks.

I should have spent more (some?) time
reflecting on all the ways I came up short.
Instead I dwelt on God tricking me,
and the girl not being right.
It was all stupid.
Of course a person learns a lot
going through such an ordeal.
If nothing else discovering who you are
as you witness your flubbed responses.

Ashamed of how I reacted,
convinced had I known
she could, and would, chart her own course
   I would never have bothered her.
I never thought she was free,
I thought she was as bound as I was.
Each of us is at liberty to believe what we like,
but we don't have any right to oblige another
to follow our interpretation of a prophecy
   (crafted by the Absolute to be baffling).
      Even supposing I did finally figure it out
      I only did so by errors spread over decades.

      Of course if we're looking for transgressions
         I was mad at the Absolute
      and that was yesterday.
      There's little conviction in my compliance,
         zero discernable contrition.
      I can't get over being suckered. Trusting.
      Why did it have to be this contorted?
      Maybe I'm unable to see my arrogance,
         or the level of my insubordination.

I lacked something

No wife
No children
There's all of humanity.

Surely a vast number
over the generations
have fallen in love
with someone they couldn't marry.
A large group - with attachment
but something intruded to block it.

What about those who felt emotion
surging in them when young,
then it turned out to be merely a stage,
the love drying to a peel,
sentenced to stay together.
Isn't that an awful punishment -
  canceling the brief good?

The millions who never had children
   - for whatever reasons.
The millions who die alone

Maybe the emotionally suffocated
are a silent majority
   or close to it.

So I join the ranks of all these

I feel God coerced this poem.
   Think what you like,
I believe it was wrung out of me.

The big picture: its never anyone's fault,
   in Life things happen.
   They can't be predictable,

and the variables must include
   the wide range of people,
   the kinds of occurrences.
I may even mature to the extent
   that I appreciate my good fortune.
   Not merely because my life was spared,
     but for all I was endowed with
       (I was given a lot).
There is always a cost.
So I've paid the cost. Albeit unwittingly.
But if this understanding comes
it will only come as I approach three score ten.
I won't get any credit for it, I don't deserve any.
   It will be like a pension one receives
   merely for surviving X number of years.

       I don't have to feel guilty about the girl.
       The reason is the result:
          she isn't stuck with some old guy.
       One dragging all the problems and troubles
          of the world in behind him.
       As a general rule one should chose true love,
       but all rules have exceptions,
          and I'd certainly qualify as one.
          I am the loser. No young wife.
             She lucked out.

             I don't think it would have occurred
                even to Sherlock Holmes himself
                   (until after the fact)
             that 'freeze' could apply to one's intended.
             I saw 'creep' and 'freeze' as slow,
                as in contrast to flare's quickness.
             Which wasn't entirely wrong, the mistake
                was giving it too much emphasis.
             Speed of light doubled was another trick.
             Not fantastic acceleration as I thought,
                but a return to normal time.

However egocentric I've come across
in the particulars of this narrative
I hope you will accept my word
that I would never imagine
my happiness as of any importance
weighed against the existence of a child.
I'm vain - but not that narrow or mean.

          Often what I've taken at first
             as an added feature
          that made something imperfect,
          I later realized
          is actually what made it perfect.
          I know the *ideal* often isn't.
          Someone with a background
             might not have worked,
          and an ordinary girl who only felt
          an abstract subconscious attraction
             might have been better.

Conservative and 'normal'
    can be wonderful too.
I can see that.
And nothing is more important
    than mother and child.

                I'm really not as irrational
                as all this makes me out to be.

          The thought occurs
            that one of the lessons might have been
            that I gave beauty too great a value.
            Yet there are women in our little area
            whose beauty is the light of goodness
            emanating from their soul.

Two opposing analyses I have no answer for:
The rationalist, 'It was all predictable.
   This is where blind faith leaves you,
    - stuck in a dead end, no way to escape.'
The other (which my higher self joins),
   'No, it wasn't faith, blind or otherwise.
   It was clinging to your fabricated fantasy.
   So when reality arrived it was traumatic.
   The anointed had a baby. So what?'
In the end I don't even know
if the pure being test was true,
or something else I just made up.

I was so screwed-up that part of the condition
was losing the awareness of *how* screwed-up.
So there could be this huge break
between my expectations,
   miraculous love and literary success,
and what my character deserved,
a true love that wasn't sure and nothing.

                        I couldn't finish this with the girl

All who retreat into the imaginary
lured by their particular lotus
   choosing escape over the real
will wake
   whether to the old opium den,
   skid row alley,
   or today's abandoned building,
shattered
   awakening to the harshest environments
Isn't this justice?
Individuals who kept making excuses
   blaming life   blaming others.
They should be held accountable
choosing illusion
   that brief reprieve satisfied

they must pay
(and get returned to the continuum).
There aren't different rules for escapists.
No one's allowed to avoid
the world all of us must share.
Its short-sighted and selfish to try.

    My submission isn't clean

        My description of her hasn't been fair.
        She had a visible tender softness
        towards what - or those - she cared for.
        I didn't know at the time
        - found out only afterwards,
        that cancer ran in her family;
        an impetus to start childbearing early.
        She had strength, but that's a good.
        Considering her background and pride
        there wasn't a trace of meanness in her.
        She wasn't the type, had she known,
        to mark an admirer's crushing as a 'triumph'.
        Even done accidentally
            it would have upset her.

            As crazy as it was
            being mad at God
            made more sense
            than being mad at a girl
            who didn't know anything.

Though I had Croesus's example to warn me
I ended up not one whit smarter.
In fact the smug overconfidence, the spiritual conceit,
were surprisingly (appallingly) duplicative.
    [Off the subject a bit
    you should read about Cyrus's death.
        I've often thought about it.
    A man as 'great' in his world and time

as Caesar and Napoleon were in theirs.
Worthy enough to be in the Bible – Isaiah 45:
   "Thus says the Lord to Cyrus his anointed".
Yet hubris also overtook him in his turn.
For no reason whatsoever he crosses a river
   to fight and conquer a strange people,
     led by a widowed queen Tomyris,
       and that's the end of him.
As the Lydians had considered the Persians primitive,
so the Persians considered the Massagetae primitive.
Its worth reading all of Herodotus - its fascinating.
   The first historian.
Though Thucydides, his only competition, denigrates
his work as collecting and retelling ancient tales.]
I could plead youth, but I wasn't that young,
   certainly not for most of the 40 years.
Where is the evidence of any spiritual growth?
My wary decisions appear sluggish and passive.
If you'd told me in my 20's
that by some miracle (series of miracles)
   I would be alive in my 60's,
I would have hoped - imagined - someone wise.
   Made so by experience.
Slower moving, but sure, a 'centered' adept.
Hopefully compassionate, benevolent - all that.
Having the visage of someone who smiles,
   though wise speaks little,
understanding the limits
   of what can be verbally transplanted.
Yet when he speaks, with an appreciative attitude
   as wide as the earth, people listen.
Having a sense of humor
   - a sage can laugh and 'sport' –
   but no longer immature or antagonistic.
The enlightened me would have been guided
   in sorting, never (or rarely) mistaken.
Confident with ample reason.
What did we actually end up with?

I've learned some things. One can't help to.
But I've fallen absurdly short of sagacity.
Not that bright, not that much smarter,
   with a lot of the goodness worn off.
     I didn't rise above myself,
     didn't shed confusion,
     didn't achieve certainty.
We have a nut who got mad at God and fate,
and denounced an innocent girl as a changeling.
That's as far from enlightenment as you can get.

                         I don't believe
                         that I'm right
                         and God's wrong

     I couldn't let go of that idealized figure I created,
     the imaginary true love which does not exist.
     The real true love does, but I don't want her.

                    I'm sure I did something wrong,
                       or didn't do something right.

          Lately, in a more complete way I think,
             I've reversed the way I look at everything.
          This poem (maybe all of my writing)
          as part of Providence's plan.
          It all had to happen the way it did
             so I'd write this the way I've written it.

Cognizant of what I'm doing,
depositing a huge heavy obstacle
   in the middle of this book.
now for some inexplicable reason
   content - happy about it.

        Providence knew what I didn't,
        that if they stalled long enough,
        stretched the pursuit over decades,

    eventually not only the ambition
    of the great personifying triumph,
    but even the appeal of wife and children
       would space away.

I need to reiterate something I mentioned earlier
as part of my initial reaction to the prophecy,
calculating that if it turned out real I'd have to measure up,
that there were bound to be some standards, boundaries.
And as I told you I was confident I could qualify.
As I've laid out all my doubts, things I guessed wrong about
    - perceptions and interpretations
(if you remember nothing else about this saga
    it'll probably be all the things I got wrong.)
Yet for some reason I need you to know
that that self-confidence never waivered.
You're free to find this insupportable and delusional,
but there it is. It is a fact. I still feel it.
    Whatever my problems I'm clay that's not so dumb
       that it isn't aware of how its being worked.
If you have the belief – the sense
that you were shaped to handle a specific job,
    perform, fulfill a certain role,
is it surprising that you would feel you could do it?

                      I used to identify myself with the new.
                      Bringing a new perspective.
                      Even a revolutionary/visionary one.
                      Now, in spite of myself, I endure as a
                      figure evoking a vanished scary world
                      people want to believe never existed,
                      where a wild Supernatural threatened
                          like shifting dark thunderclouds
                      to suddenly intervene into the human.

    It has occurred to me
       that my life
       in this telling

will make more sense to you
than it ever did to me
while I was living through it.

      Yes I wanted that love so close
      where both care more about the other.
      I wanted children. I love children.
      to discover how the blend comes out.
      Enjoyment and excitement
          expanded by fear
      that ultimate never-ending attachment.
      Why should I apologize for a desire
      so natural that it comes with our bodies?
      (Even if today many, with their minds ruling,
      survey the hassles and obligations of children,
      turned off, firmly decide: that's not for me.)

      Yet as the years rolled on
      whereas once I had only imagined
      love and blissful happiness,
      now I dwelt on all that could go wrong.
      So many divorces. Relations can sour.
      There's no predicting.
      We've all seen once devoted couples
          get fed up and turn on each other.
      Then you think how with age
      the risk of birth defects and autism rise.
      The possibility that you won't see anything
      in your child you can identify with.
      You will love them of course,
      but their character could be entirely alien.
      And there's no control over how children develop.
      If you don't feel a connection
      you might resent all the time they require.
      You want them to have a spark
          but there are no guarantees.

> Those repeating unstoppable phrases
> that kept erupting from the depths
> (so far, thankfully, only breaking forth
> when I'm alone, so even if muttered
>   going unobserved),
> slowed in frequency and vehemence,
> mostly 'No one loves me',
> now were joined by:
>   'I don't deserve anything. Nothing.'
>   'I'm a terrible person'.
>   'Poor Mom – stuck with a loser.'
> I know that as behavioral tics
> they're still signs - symptoms of cracking.
> Yet in their content I can't help but see
> a relatively positive turn and development
>   in taking responsibility,
> moving away from self-pity and playing
>   with stupid unexamined conviction,
>   the ambushed innocent.
> I can anticipate a day now
> when these exclamations cease.

The last countermove I contemplated
was to take *when in heaven* literally,
intentionally miss the metaphorical usage -
push to have the truth be (to have always been)
that fulfillment must wait until the next world.
In the unlikely event that this tactic was successful
it ran the risk that I'd wear the *creep* tag in perpetuity,
no longer a humorous dig at a guy too old
    for involving a girl too young,
but a serious brand on a hard-hearted villain
    for spurning that same girl.
Of course the fact that I didn't literally die in a flare
undercut the prospect of convincing myself;
an essential first step in the process of making it real.

The last twist my thought took
was a rationalization meant to reassure
yet whose logic you had to wonder about:
'Its obvious you wanted a different outcome.
That makes your rejection of everything okay.'

Occasionally during the worst period
   - a couple of years –
I would mutter, "I don't want to live anymore."
These weren't those uncontrollable utterances,
they were childish, but conscious declarations,
   as if to register a change of heart
   to a monitoring authority.
Yet at other times I would respond strongly
against any thoughts of death
with the self-reprimanding condemnation:
   "I'm a quitter."
Later, when the despair lows wore away,
I would remind myself that whatever my problems
I was in a much better state than I had been.

I had taken the common phrase
'big as you please' in
round about the freeze
was as big as you please
as some throwaway line exaggeration,
possibly derisive of something or someone (me?)
With 'round about' being another common phrase,
their force seemed weakened by generalization.
Now though I think it could infer
   - whatever freeze means in this iteration -
that its duration depends on my disposition.

Another thing I reconsidered late
and changed my mind about, was my initial take
   on remembering the trichinosis lines.
I had presumed Providence was mocking, as pathetic,
my resort to the consolations in the next world,

the built-in positives Existence has for every misfortune;
compensations like appreciation, motivation, liberation.
As I said I was musing that in lieu of the singular love
   - wife, children, ties that last forever,
the alternative might be complete freedom,
somewhat akin to the openness with which we start life.
(Its never good versus bad, superior versus inferior.
While the options are opposite, both are good.
Those who received something concrete
have a relationship which can never be taken away.
Those who were deprived here are free to move
without the gravity of an eternal relationship,
   in a field not impinged by what was given.)
I could see now that it had only been coincidence
   that when I recalled that strange augury
- prompted by the perversity of a fate that ended
with the promised love employed in a mortuary,
I also happened to be contemplating
   those thoughts of self-solace.
Its helpful to remember the young man I was
at the time I received that mocking speech,
   the fullness of my delusional conceit.
Believing myself a figure of destiny,
and having discovered material reality's malleability,
I presumed that (unseen), by will and thought alone,
I could bend what occurred to outcomes I preferred.
Providence, using my own sarcastic voice, described
the conundrum I would actually face down the road,
imprisoned, pacing, buried alive in my own tomb,
an official religious monument to human sacrifice.
It was the presumption I had then that was the target,
not my later self-consoling thoughts about heaven.

The perspective age affords
when I think back on that period
of intoxicated ego, my conception
that I could conduct manifestation,
determine what would rise and fall;

the prime example of that extreme delusion
was thinking I could make the prophecy
   apply when and to whom I decided.
Obliged to remember the fiasco that resulted.
But what strikes me now
(whether irony is the right term or not)
is how similar that course was
to the one the anointed love would follow
   - forty years later.
Illusion or true, it didn't seem to matter.
Yes there were significant differences.
The first: all avenues came to dead-ends,
   and no connections were ever allowed.
Poles never aligned – always repulsed.
The attraction itself came from secret pain
neither could ever acknowledge or divulge.
And the doomed hope was spread out,
   with a can't-let-go aspect.
Whereas with the second reenactment
connection was theoretically possible,
   just prevented.
There was only one (huge) surprise
   - so the end was abrupt and final.
(Mutual recognition coming in its wake.)
A chance pregnancy with no chance to it.
God knowing I wouldn't touch her.
A young girl who would appear unworthy
put forward as what I deserved, and needed,
and who would be worthy (after this ordeal).
In both cases I accept the fault was mine.
Forcing the prophecy to fit was a violation
   that received the stomping it deserved;
and the lack of compassion with the second,
   justified its already-included punishment.
Yet I mean it when I say that what hits me now
   are not the differences - but the similarities.
The weird wrong-footing timing both featured,
   which was absolutely uncorrectable.

The atmosphere of uncertainty.
Large misunderstandings a beat later exposed.
Even the feeling after the end was the same,
not just loss and hurt, but deprivation:
   a glimpsed promised perfect union,
   the compulsion to complete something
   that could never be completed.
Finally telling yourself you must leave off.

     In my conception of heaven
     we will be 'times' ourselves,
        our souls consolidated - comprehension increased.
     The freedom there - the great powers granted -
     simply from our minds to create
        and control matter that is real and solid
        (unlike the empty stuff that surrounds us here).
     Yet while smarter, happier, empowered,
     we still must be who we are.
     Therefore I expect we'll roll through different moods
        and I anticipate my own occasional regrets.
     My defense of my behavior here, beyond the expected,
       'I gave my life to Art' or 'the pursuit of truth'
       will be to slant the narrative so I appear
       more struggling innocent than calculating perpetrator
       (this poem could foretell such an attempt),
       I was so sensitive, how could I recover
       from the relentless series of psychic surprises?
     My confidence in this representation isn't strong.
     What comeback can I muster to the glib snipes,
       'Why can't you just admit you messed up?'
       'You misread your oracle. Whose fault is that?'
     Furthermore why couldn't anyone who ever lived
     offer a post-traumatic-stress excuse for their life?
       'Starting with the shock of birth it was too much.
       Existing – how inexplicable is that?
       Suddenly the world confronts you
         - all these things that already exist
       including other living creatures. Including people.

    And everything keeps changing. Why?
    I struggled to swim to the surface - of the dream -
    while partially hypnotized, partially paralyzed,
    but couldn't manage it. I could never cope'
I'd buy it. Or say I did. I'd be obliged to wouldn't I?

      In the next world, with our wider enhanced vision,
      when we look back at life on Earth as done,
        with an enlightened peaceful understanding
      we'll see that it all had to be as it was.
      As a composition it had to be cut into these divisions,
        to work, and it happened to fall where it fell.
      Even if individually we got hurt
        everyone's existence depends on the whole.
      I also expect, that for those of us
        with a soul worthy of the name,
      we will see everyone as family,
          as brother or sister
          father or mother
          daughter or son.
      With greater comprehension
      able to follow, in ourselves and others,
      the extreme shifts in age and shapes
      that beings there can metamorphize through,
      we'll be able to fathom multiple relationships.

God wants a sacrifice that means something.
   True love would qualify.
   Children.
   Your whole life.

            I believe I act as I've told you. When it seems
              an instruction is from the Absolute
            it never occurs to me to do anything
            except obey (like a well-broken dog).
            It was just that I was caught so off-guard
              when the challenge turned out backloaded
                the true love far from solely a reward

    the heart of the hardest passage.
Surprised (after being worn out),
    hurt and angry,
and yes possessed of the wrong nature,
I quit.
So when it counted I failed on obedience.
On the other hand what if I passed
    on discernment and faith?
This could be more self-deception.
Discernment
    Reflecting on interpretations and keys.
    Very little of the prophecy was explicit.
    I'd 'die' in a flare, there'd be a 'freeze'
       (of indeterminate application),
    and I was in for it.
    The conjectures of my imagination
    were influenced by the personal:
       preconceptions, needs & desires.
    I may have captured the '2' designation
    but I molded it into an image of the ideal,
       perfect match, irresistible bond force;
    which obviously left out – missed - a lot.
    I felt privileged receiving the prophecy
       - special inside knowledge -
    when the whole point of its effect
    may have been to make
       a contrived 'accident' irreparable.
    I decided, entirely on my own,
    that the 'other half' would have to be
    someone spiritual gifted in some way,
    or possessed of a rare literary sensibility.
    (I thought of those as intrinsic qualities,
    when they might have constituted
       a kind of knowledge
    that would have made the love impure.)
    I scanted other possibilities,
    never imagining that it could be
    a completely innocent normal person.

That poor girl. All my expectations.
My fear of making a mistake.
The 'pure being recognition test' idea.
I had five years to make an adjustment,
    but never did.
Because of its length it was natural
to assume the trial was about endurance.
When in the end it switched to character
    - my character - my weaknesses -
all I could manage was anger.
Yet if it had all rolled as I expected
it wouldn't have proven anything.
Before I decided I had gotten too old
I placed all the blame on the girl
for making the wrong selection.
But the Absolute blamed me,
for failing to cope with that wrinkle.

Faith
    Not really knowing what you believe
until it doesn't happen.
What sort of person says,
    'God can keep his girl.'?
Appalling discoveries.
I had set conditions. Unacceptable.
Deep in my core was a fundamentalist
pronouncing who was unworthy
(hidden in that denunciation of course
    was the assertion that *he* was worthy).
Some time after the blow wore off
I should have gathered myself,
assessed everything that had happened,
summoned the integrity to acknowledge
that the Whole knew better what was best
- not just for my small self, but for everyone.
The truth is I never came back.
    I never recovered.
I fell into my standard division,
head conceding what it had to concede,

        heart having no part of it.
        So I had no part of it.
        If you really believe things – resultant reality
           ends up – has to be as it is,
        which is what I profess (even to myself),
        how do I explain my righteous indignation
        when events contradicted my expectations?
        Its pretty funny. I was so confident
        that I would demonstrate my faith,
        and what I ended up showing
        was that my faith was worthless.
        Obedience might be my strong suit.

    I know this is all incredible.
    I wouldn't believe it
    if I happened to read it.

Croesus should have stopped, made sure
   the doomed empire was the Persian.
He didn't - out of over confidence.
Regarding himself as pious,
sure Apollo and the other gods
agreed with his estimation of his own merit,
   he counted on their favor.
What the trichinosis lines underscored to me,
what Croesus, broken, was forced to learn,
   is that no one escapes their fate.
No matter how smart you think you are.
No matter how pious you think you are.
My eager interpretation that the prophecy
   promised true love and success,
was, like Croesus's, built atop vanity.
A narcissistic inflation of self-worth.
Had events aligned with my interpretation
it would have made me even more arrogant.

        I didn't put it together

> I never grasped, while it still mattered,
> that beyond any incidents, any developments,
> I had been 'in deep' in the past,
> was 'in deep' in the present,
> and would always be 'in deep'.
> And it wasn't a sentence of doom,
> it was actually the rarest blessing.

> When do I see
> what I'm supposed to see?

A person reaches a certain age
if they have normal sense, a normal soul,
their circumstances haven't been especially bad,
they should come to accept their life.
Realize how large their own contribution was
   to whatever happened to them.
How important each period in their life was.
So it is with me, despite the rejecting resentment,
the reluctance to relent to what the World served
   as fait accompli existential circumstantial
the seeker inside (balancing) finally accedes.
While there was a correction of ego
the recovery was more a case
of Being coming forward and taking over.
   The lesson sinks in
that in the end what a person doesn't have
   isn't them.
What they do have – is.

> The splendor of life is inexhaustible,
> in - on its dimensions and facets
> we will spend eternity meditating
> and like an endless fountain spring
> it will keep flowing
>   meaning joy wonder
>   always rewarding.
> But the astonishing fact

       of our particular existence - identity
       comes down to who we are
          because that's the gift
       and we should make peace with it.

    I'm sorry I wasn't grateful.
    But I got my hopes up

the answer to 'Why would God do this to me?'
   in all this I think I finally understand.

Forgive me World.
If I can remember what's important
   maybe I can get it together.

good advice   I could never take

UNPATRIOTIC

I think I've lost my patriotism.
I'm not happy about this development
   regarding it as another defeat.
Its appalling to be unsure if you love your own country.
   What if you think they've gone bad though?
   How can one say he loves his country
   if he no longer loves his countrymen?
     And do I?
Most Americans of course aren't guilty of anything
   beyond willful ignorance and indifference
Still, under oath could I swear I loved my country?
And it is unnatural -
   like souring on your own family.
What can I do?

I used to be patriotic. I hope you'll take my word.
I loved the American Revolution.
I loved the whole colonial period. Pored over everything.
American Heritage magazine.
Read all of Bruce Catton on the Civil War.
Gloried in our World War II triumphs.
Accepted the Whitmanesque example to the world.
Believed we'd grown, and would keep improving.
I knew and sang all the service songs:
   'From the halls of Montezuma..'
   'Off we go into the wild blue yonder...'
   'Anchors away my boys, anchors away...'
   'And it's 1 2 3 in the field artillery...'
   'You'll never get rich digging a ditch,
     you're in the army now...'

It was the burden of Vietnam I think
   that eventually wore it all down and away.
When we turned into Antiochus
   "You, lowly subjects, will bow down to my power
     - or you will die!"

years of napalm, B-52 carpet bombing, 'free fire zones',
    then in all the years that followed stonewalling
    No national repentance for great crimes, only denial.
Regret for our losses and trauma,
    not for what we had done.

It had been an unknown land with an unknown past,
jungles inhabited by some backward inscrutable Asians.
Their peasants getting recruited into being communists,
    joining the opposing team en masse.
If we couldn't slaughter them who could we slaughter?
Our assignment was to maintain control of most of the earth.
History wasn't relevant, reality wasn't relevant.
The hidden history was that in Vietnam the French
had violated all their principles and their own revolution,
then (like the Brits had always done) lied to themselves.
We, after picking up the tab at the end for the French,
would follow their example,
violating all our principles and our revolution.

In the decades that followed
we never honestly confronted what we'd done.
An actor president, on his way to complete dementia,
recast the intervention as a 'noble cause',
as if factuality could be changed if you altered the script.
As if millions slain no longer weighed against us.
There was no conscience
about the world's most advanced country
murdering the inhabitants of one of the poorest.
It had been a crusade against communism!
Never mind that to the average patriotic Vietnamese
capitalism and communism had very little meaning.
All they saw were Western aliens,
acting in the same way as their old European overlords,
working with the same turncoats
  - Christians in a Buddhist country -
who had worked for the French.
Arrogantly we assumed it was apparent to all

that we were the best people, with the best system,
that we were only there to keep them on the right track:
   'Want to be a free entrepreneur? Of course you do.
   We'll pay you to fight, but repeat this oath -.'

Though I've forgotten everything else
about the North Hollywood Induction Center
I'll never forget the bank of older Republican women
the conformity behind that raised counter,
all with the same round sprayed stiff hair
in unnaturally colored dyes,
busy processing grandson aged boys.
   Sternly serious, all business
intent on their patriotic duty
shuffling papers that determined lives.
      channeling kids to death, or to be killers.
These women had imbibed all the propaganda,
the conflict was like World War II...
        Fight the enemy - with courage.
        Its your turn.
        Be a man.
If I hadn't seen it myself I couldn't have imagined it,
not the exaggerated details of something so perverse.
Facially they were of a similar type too,
   must have been very pretty when young.
Even now they were Norman Rockwell grandmothers,
   sterotypes found on food packages or greeting cards.
Except in grim reality they worked for a death factory.
If this was a righteous American crusade for freedom
   there was no excuse for shirking your duty.
Everything in the world had changed
but they weren't given the faculties to grasp that.

   The poor of the earth,
   fascinated by our affluent lifestyle,
   saw us as a huge swaggering bully
      throwing his weight around.
   Lying to himself but fooling no one else.

A point the punctilious Selective Service made was that
you couldn't receive Conscientious Objector status
unless you opposed all wars (maybe all violence?)
At the time I thought this typical arbitrary abuse
  by an authoritarian bureaucracy biased towards evil.
Slowly, after many years, I've come to see its sense,
    even if as a policy rule.
If we grant to the state the right to conscript
how can we allow such an easy dodge as:
  'Well I happen to oppose this particular conflict'?
I wasn't then - I've never been - a complete pacifist.
Though I've always admired that purity and conviction,
looked up to it as a higher morality, superior to my own.
    But like my father I would have volunteered
        to fight the despicable fascists;
    fully aware that the enemy soldier I killed
    was just like myself – one other human being
    caught up in something bigger than himself.
Even if I couldn't say *I believe in* self-defense,
    I knew I'd resort to it.
In the extremely unlikely event that a foreign nation
disabled our computers,
  decapitated command and control,
and then occupied us (out of fear of a counterattack),
I would join the armed resistance.

As much as I admired the principles and forthrightness
of the young men who went to prison,
  and even those who fled to Canada,
who, in contrast to me, thought things through,
civil disobedience   moral example
        non-violent public protest,
I could never understand the underlying rationale.
Because it seemed as if they were acknowledging
  the power and authority of the killers and liars.
As if vermin could lawfully take over the United States.
        No!
I never for a second considered them legitimate.

We're not required to cede anything to snakes.
Usurpers may have their day,
   glory in their bloody spoils,
   that is the way of the world.
But we grant them nothing but the curse of heaven,
   their very existence a blight on good.

Though I tend to view veteran's organizations
as fonts for ever more nationalism/militarism
some of the nicest couples I've ever known
were involved with them as their social vortex.
   (My parents resided for several years
   at a California veteran's home
   established after the Civil War.)
And who wouldn't find associations attractive
   that exist to honor you?

Its indelicate today to note that many enlist
   primarily as a vocational option.

      The memorialization of fighting
      always ends in the next killing   pre-justified

The guys I've known who saw heavy combat
   didn't want to talk about it
      what had happened haunted them.
They'd never consider joining a veteran's group
the idea of parading in uniform dress up,
recounting the violence endlessly,
   regaling others with it - as if a tale
would strike them as twisted.
Of course many vets never saw action
and I guess even for some who did
   enough years pass
      memories are malleable
you scant the trembling fear — the terror
the inescapableness of facing pitiless Death
that confrontation

             very real – close upon you
         the horror of risking your life - of killing;
the dreadfulness of the unmoving bodies.
Emphasize what you miss,
those moments when adrenaline fully awakened
         quickened your senses.
It can all get converted into stories
- part tragedy and drama for weight -
through which our hero passes: emerges.
     The young may not know
     that those who talk most
     are often compensating
     for having done the least,
         been the least.

                    I would not want any true hero
                        deprived of honor he had earned.
                    Defending your people is still a virtue
                        with a noble heritage.
                    Yet we know what these ceremonies reinforce,
                    and we know how frequently in our age
                        the killings are arbitrary, even mistaken.

Battle through the ages has always been recalled
wistfully by survivors
     long after the horror has grown cold,
     the fear and gore only evoked for effect
background to a thrilling test
     where/when a man could prove himself.
     Told by one who happened to live.
     A prettied past which sentenced its dweller
     to reside in shadow.
What can't be forgiven though
     is the conscienceless recruitment of the young
     to convince them that this path is good
         to risk their own death   to deal death.

Those who mold/hold as their identity,
    their years on 'active duty'
are similar (when not the same people)
     to those whose emotional lives climaxed
    during their school years.
    All the strongest feelings of love,
    peaking with physical agility and strength.
    Unable to leave that time behind
    though the calm years that stretch afterwards,
    when they're wiser and more stable,
      are far vaster.
    We can't say its unnatural
    since its gauged to the body's prime
      for attraction and breeding.
    Still...

            The Empire eyes the world as its property
            and fears prospective rivals.
            Strategists skulk and plot at the top,
            tapping the great power of the state.
            War-profiteers derive great wealth from -
            but take no responsibility for - the carnage.
            Officers who will spin for escalation
              (this is their business – fighting,
                when a career can really be made).
            Hawks, inside and outside, will always
            fear-monger and agitate for any war.
            Many not keen to risk their own lives
            have no hesitation in jeopardizing others'.
            There are dire warnings if we don't act.
            Rosy predictions if we do.
            Once intervention is launched
              it'll be: "Support the troops!"
            When it starts to go bad they'll wind:
              "Don't let their sacrifice be for naught."
            The advocates of war have nothing to fear
              from reversal and collapse.
            Since they always ask for too much,

             their counter is prepared:
             'We were hampered, not totally committed.
                Now you can see the result.'

             To "We should honor those who served."
             We must respond, "Well of course,
                and those who've been wounded."
             Decency demands it.
             Comprehensive care for our wounded,
                - physical and mental.
             But nothing will make the violence right
             or the suffering of all parties less tragic.

        Consider war as an end in itself
        separated from any supposed cause.

I've known a few radicals who you could say
   really did hate the U.S.
But they were always a tiny segment of the left,
and what they hated were not our people
but our nation becoming a vulgar surly Goliath
   forcing his way anywhere he wanted,
   families of those resisting
      soon cast into mourning.
   A bully who took whatever he wanted,
   stomped on those who didn't jump.
   Giant who also had the insolent gall
   to declare that he had God's blessing.
But most radicals made a distinction,
and loved our country, loved our people.
The plutocrats are few, far away,
   unknown, presumed without souls.
True they have the power to sow confusion,
exploit fear and hate
   from those with fear and hate in them.
And their hirelings and goons on their orders
   can physically block the good.
But in the biggest complete picture

    the criminal and damned,
    the manipulated and purchased,
      are also victims with their shriveled souls.
Radicals are usually idealists, not just zealots.
Reaching to better the common welfare,
motivated in this direction out of a passion
    for humanity's plight.
My parents for example had a pure patriotism,
a love of America and our people.
Like many on the left, it was free of chauvinism.
    As a child I'd study them
when one of our patriotic songs was sung.
If it was a moving rendition
   goose bumps would form on their arms
   and their eyes would fill.

They didn't ignore how people were misled,
but they believed in their basic goodness
       - in everyone
if you could only get through to them
tell them how things really stood
    you could trust them
   their innate decency and common sense
   to eventually chose - and do - what was right.

I was always more leery.
   As with everything else
this is saturated with irony,
since my parents were skeptics,
    wholly political;
while I gave primacy to the spiritual,
believing (then and now) that everyone's core
     their soul
   is a fabric-part of God.
So presumably I should be the one to avow
a faith in people, our 'brothers and sisters'.
Yet I would no more rely on them
   than I would cats and dogs.

> In our family 'walking door to door'
> during political campaigns
> was an essential rite
> which proved your commitment.
> Your belief in people, in democracy.
> It was effective, it was grassroots;
> it demonstrated your willingness to stand up,
> do something that made a difference.
> It took the measure of what you were.
> I hated it. Always dreaded it.
> Though I never doubted it was a valid gauge,
> and felt guilty about shirking
> > my good citizen's duty.
> Precinct lists in hand,
> usually only visiting registered Democrats,
> it still had about it the uninvited intrusion
> > of salesmen pushing a product
> > or proselytizers pushing their religion.
> Yes we were better informed,
> and we were acting for the general good,
> not anything self-aggrandizing
> > (if you don't count being right).
> Still the posture and confident insistence
> had the taint of superior know-it-alls.

Its not that I believe Americans are bad.
Like my parents I believe we're good.
But we are vulnerable
to the intrigues of the connivers
because of that toxic mix
of glutted arrogance & willful ignorance.
> 'Hey if it was really important
> I'd know it already, wouldn't I?'
Susceptible to the crudest propaganda
consenting to invade countries
they couldn't locate on a geographic atlas,
let alone tell you anything about the people,
their culture or history.

The worship of their strange idols
>Money
>Guns
>Conquest/Military Might,
an unquestionable faith that we're always right,
>we don't ever make mistakes;
We were made best, have done best,
>have nothing to learn from other nations;
leads to an authoritarian allegiance,
a dark creed's groupthink of blind obedience.
Better not question totalitarian 'security'
>or imperial strikes.

Suspect to them are programs that help & care
for elderly, prisoners, minorities, or the poor.
They've trademarked 'Christian', like a brand.
If you swear that Jesus is God - God's Son,
>you're in, you get to wear the team uniform.
Don't sweat spirituality, charity, or good works.
Everything's literal and primitive;
>baptism and Eucharist are magic rites.
The fact that the religion's nominal founder
was obviouly an extreme pacifist is ignored,
somehow (for centuries) deemed not relevant.
>Nice guy. Too nice.
'Love your enemy'?
They're incapable of loving their 'neighbor'.

They snarl at any proposal to recompense
the descendants of the people whose blood
>we spilled on our soil;
the Blacks, whose stolen labor built the country,
or the American Indians, whose stolen land
>is the country.
They have contempt for the very idea.
We must keep quiet as Confederates lecture us
on their (barbarous) notion of nationalism,

and threaten an armed resistance insurrection
should we scrutinize their stockpile of guns,
or even consider a fairer tax on the rich.
'American Exceptionalism' excuses
economic and military world dominion.
Patriotism comes down to the willingness to kill
in order to subjugate foreign people
who have somehow stupidly gotten in our way,
and obstinately won't obey our directives.
God favors dog-eat-dog capitalism
    (and needless to say White people)
so naturally He blesses
    our economic and military rule.
If you are so perverse as to suggest out loud that
the heathens might have a legitimate grievance,
possibly even some reason to hate us (US),
they point at you as if you've just confessed
    some an inner rot of unAmericanism.
This from crackpot haters seething with treason,
people who go nuts over any humane proposal
    (like medical coverage for everyone),
yet somehow magically retain the exclusive right
to be the 'real Americans' and 'true Christians'.

If we discount for all the knowledge
earlier civilizations were closed off from,
that we are handed with little effort,
it seems inconceivable
that any earlier people ever existed
as their area and age's dominant power
who could have been as stupid as we are.
They wouldn't have survived.
  Not the Chinese
      Egyptians
      Persians
      Greeks
      Romans
      Mongols

      Arabs
      French
      Turks
      British
I'm talking about real intelligence -
awareness of who you are, where you are,
who others are, what is actually happening.
The Romans didn't elect Caligula or Nero;
    but we did elect and reelect Nixon, Reagan,
      and the younger Bush.
    We've always considered ourselves the child
    of classicism's democratic republicanism
      - hence the style of our public buildings.
    But we're probably closer to our German cousins,
    specifically the mob that abandoned democracy,
      captured/brainwashed/reprogrammed/robotic.
    Maybe most of us are not as cold-blooded,
    less willing to commit the murders ourselves,
      but then we don't have to.

Today people betraying our founding ideals
  obstreperous in vulgar jingoism
treat the flag in ways
  nailing it to walls
  leaving it out all night, in all types of weather
  letting it trail on the ground
things we were taught in the Cub Scouts
  never to allow.
Which even now as a non-cultist, I wouldn't.

    I held onto the flag, wouldn't let go,
    the one we received when Dad passed away
      for his World War II service

        As in the Yeatsian omen 'the worst'
          really are filled with passionate certainty.
        Hypocrites assume the office of arbiter.
        If you won't publicly assent

to their childish version of God
then you don't believe in God.
If you don't share
   their childish version of Jesus
then you aren't a Christian.
And their perversion of patriotism
   is as irrational and deviant.
Standing for what the Founders opposed,
   what the British empire represented.
Police state surveillance is justified,
   rights trumped by security needs.
For themselves however
   there's a schizophrenic escape clause.
They are free to cast the same government
they employ overseas as a Superpower enforcer
   as a specter of a coming domestic tyrant.
They stir themselves up to fake paranoia,
   pretend they are persecuted,
while every year cheating on their taxes.

Enough years pass and you quit the contest.
Telling yourself its only surrendering names
whose meanings have been co-opted anyway.
It isn't true. You've written people off.
Which is of course a violation.
One isn't permitted to decide a whole multitude
   has nothing inside them worthwhile.
Dispite your recoiling antipathy you know this.
You've also judged the meek majority,
whose humanity and soul you don't question,
as too stupid to cut their way through
   all the falsehoods set up to steer them.

The widening rift grows into a vale.
It looks as if their mouths are moving
but you can no longer make out any words.
Far from disturbing, its a pleasant outcome.
Though you sense the ethics are shaky.

> What a relief to be spared dirtying yourself,
> wasting 'quality time' deciphering their noise,
> and charting its simplistic psychological veins.

Sometimes we assume arguing,
whether kept polite and calm,
   a reasoned debate,
   or a heated shouting bout,
shows those furthest apart.
A deep, possibly permanent disagreement.
As I've gotten older I wonder
if the greatest gulfs aren't marked by silence.
There is some truth in that old bromide
that political foes are actually closer,
distinct from the majority;
because both believe the issues/decisions
- and the civic sphere itself - are important.
Argument as a testament not only to conviction
   but to respect and valuation of the endeavor.
We just can't see past our differences.
   I'm confident in being right
   and I can always blame the opposition
    '*They* were hardened in their views,
    they couldn't/wouldn't hear our position
    fairly, or consider that we might be right'.
Yet in my soul I still know
good people don't give up on anyone,
they are like Jesus, untainted by hate.

> To harp on this may sound petty
> but am I the only one who cringes
> when a group of American boosters
> at an international sports competition
> start pounding the partisan chant:
>   "USA! USA! USA!"
> in a drowning out goonish shout;
> top dog lording it over the weaker?
> If the Chinese do supercede us

                    and start behaving
                        (not that I think they would)
                    in such a vulgar boorish manner,
                    imagine how we'd react to that.
                    We don't have a brain in our heads.

To be fair
there are lots of ordinary Americans
    some of our neighbors
whose patriotism is simple and pure.
Loyalty to ones own I guess
    a natural sentiment.
Maybe a family member died in a war.

Just as we should remember
there are many Christians who are humble
who aren't filled with hypocritical evil.
Who attend church, are sincere,
help the unfortunate with humility,
strive to improve and do their best.
They're not all fakes.

On the positive: as people we're so open that
others (Europeans & Asians) find it embarrassing.
But I think it comes from friendliness and honesty.
We don't feel we have anything to hide,
and we generously assume they don't either.

                    I'm an American
                    I'm not anything else.
                    If I lived in another country
                    I'd be a foreign resident.
                    I could never become a citizen
                        that would be unthinkable.
                    You are who you are.

Maybe if I could let go of the grandiose claims
that intoxicated and inflated after World War II,
that I supposedly withstood (but obviously didn't)
our embodiment as Light of Liberty & Democracy,
example to all people and societies of living together,
a help to others in the world, not taking advantage;
and simply accept we're not better than others
      never were
I'd come to realize we're not worse either.

Its cruel
what time does to everyone

A House Made of Glass

When love is a house of glass

one day on a hillside
you discover   off on its own
an opulent gleaming mansion
built all of glass

the glittering complexity a little intimidating,
    dazzling, almost blindingly bright.
yet you are drawn to it
bewitched in a way
compelled to approach ever closer
    curious to see
     what it could be
       how it is done.

the sensation is mostly visual
until you reach the threshold
    everything's open
The exhilaration of brilliance
your emotions launch
       wonder and enthrallment as you tour
        each crystalline room ethereal
          where others might perceive emptiness
         you see perfect space and light
            with it the inspirational feeling
             of full being

                 part of it comes from memory
                 these same silent holy colors
                 when a child
                 lying on your back
                   on the grass

        fingers before your eyes
        a touch refracted the sun's ray
            the rainbow-webs came
            arrayed out stiff
        but you knew the silk was fluid
        will you ever be that free again?
        and in the sun of course
            you were warm.

then a further happy development
you see there are no checks to entrance
it seems you were expected

a peaceful magic wonder gently infuses
reassuring you that it's right.
beyond the surprising access
your emotions rise with
        Satisfaction
        arrival
        acceptance
        relief
        [exhale]
You do get carried away
to proud Justification, thinking
'At last appreciated for my true value,
my true weight and worth.
Seen - understood – admired.'
            [inhale]

Since the walls are nothing but great panes of glass
the world and the interior seem one
      (Visibility)
   you to it   they to you
You do not care in the slightest
buoyed – intoxicated by it all -
you are hospitable   without reserve
  'I have nothing to hide!
  Let everyone join in the celebration'

believing it your Consecration
the prism'd light anointing

Inside it's as warm as summer
(any gusting wind locked out)
you feel cleansed   renewed   gathered
You are ready
   in a pose of modesty
   behind it confidence
to accept your earned reward

And what of the object   the person
        of love   herself?
She 'appears'
  and appears ideal
    in beauty   attitude   taste
as if she were mixed just to match you
    (and the thought does occur)
ordained Complemental
    exactly as you appreciate everything about her
    she appreciates everything about you.
flush with Joy spreading
anticipation of apotheosis
       Ecstasy

Sunset is spectacular of course.
the yellow Sun swells at the earth's ridge
its light shared exclusively with you
gilds the face of every object.
a dispersed herd of dainty puff clouds
stenciled on the horizon
keep getting prettier, till they glow bright red.
yet already, though you try not to pick up on it,
feel a subtracting undertow of foreboding.

As high as you soared in the Day
   epiphany of life (consummation of your own)
So deep shall you fall in the Night.

doubt   as all that confirmed you,
    that you in turn politely acknowledged,
        seems to be evacuating
            like shadows stretching   then disappearing

As the Sun sinks below the horizon
light and heat go with it
    a chill in the chambered air
the forms (which in reality always stayed outside)
shrink back into themselves
smaller   motionless   fading to gray
    then disappear in the dark.
        You are alone
    It seems obvious that there was Deception.
you are prodded to recall what you've always known
glass is poor insulation.

                        Beyond the physical assault -
                            as the temperature dives
                            you find yourself on the floor
                            your body curled
                            in an instinctive defense
                            against the numbing cold
                            busy flexing spasms -
                            the realization/intimation
                            that something worse is coming
                            some ultimate humiliation.
                        for the perfect love has also vanished
                        She too was a mirage
                            a trick of ego
                        glass's hidden mirror quality
                            which took your own reflection
                            broke it through its facets
                            cleverly recombined it
                            into the image of a longed-for-one
                                beguiling   familiar   yet fresh,
                                reassuring   while intriguing.

You were enthralled
  - with yourself.
The paeans you sung
  - were to yourself.
What an embarrassing disgrace
    Shame

You can't start a fire for heat
its light would spell exposure
everyone could see you.

You can't flee either
the night has become blind blackness.
actually you can't move anyway
   as you're destroyed.

The only question that remains
Will you attempt to blame others,
or will you absorb
and acknowledge the truth?

I have been a shadow to the people I have known
and maybe even a shadow-self even to myself

Aesthetic Lenses

I'll tell you what poetry is
not anyone else
  (and yes I'll *show* you)

Personal & imaginative
  yet it must be true.
The way we say a musical note
  is right.

    the history of poetry
  before writing
recitation to the assembled
    sounding patterns echoing
    chanting nodding rhythms
  alliterative ripples
    pulsing story
      of fate
    and powers ordained.
Composed for some occasion,
  arranged representatives,
significance to impress,
in accord with tradition.

Antiquity
people in experimental spaces,
belief worked with the unknown,
  the world a more fantastical place.
Famous tales
told in turn to each generation.
  Their gods had a certain dominion
    - not just their star -
  an aspect of behavior, of experience
    phantomized identity
  they served to embody.
Of course myth-stories grow and change,
  vary for people in different places,

    alter for the times,
  while keeping their character.

Our souls have a need for tales of wonder,
evoked by voice and cadence of a spell
   - the desire to be awed.
We need to hear of individuals escaping,
  of some who surpassed.
Societies and rulers need heroes
  for practical reasons.
To rouse their people
to bravery tenacity loyalty.
      Inspirations
implanting the belief
that self-sacrifice and honor
are the highest virtues.
Will be remembered and praised.
Like bees and ants
we need members willing to die
  to benefit the colony.
Since we can't rely on instinct
  we have to indoctrinate.

The impulse to enhance
figures of the past
  as greater than ourselves,
from a time when gods fought giants
when gods mixed with mortals
  (was this true? what does it mean?)

If we don't continue to honor the fabled
  what hope can there be for us
  - that we'll be remembered?

Entrusted to a rhapsode
  "This is what I do.
    I go from city to city.
    I've memorized every line. Every word."

    sometimes he brings a musician
    for the setting to be life's beauty
        plucking a lyre
      picking
       incremental steps
      a reverie
      that spreads
     an awareness
    that every history
      is a part
    of the stream of life
      continuing
       dramatic
    naturally sentimental
     'everything passes away'

or maybe to a flute
  hollow air
    the length of breath
  enchanted alternative
    remembrance
leave today's concerns
to follow the story
with the movement of conjured memory
    an enchanted nostalgia
     'the world we knew can never return'

    Listeners stirred
       from all that's lost
       from all who've gone
    taking the adventure in
    tapping the emotion in their breast
    stoked by the teller.
    If it's a tale they've never heard
    or the reciter is exceptionally powerful
    the buildup excitement

　　　　will seem to promise
　　　　　　to contain
　　　　some great secret
　　　a revelation – a breakthrough
about? - that's never defined.
　　　couldn't be
because it would differ for everyone.
and anyway nothing like that
　　　is going to be delivered.
Deftly at the end a switch is made
　　　　to a compromise-substitute
　　　　　proven acceptable.

What makes a story truly great
　　as it weaves its way,
are the minor additions
that appear unimportant and unnecessary
　　as it ventures into the fabulous.
details that seem extraneous to the plot,
incidental objects, arbitrary occurrences,
character quirks,
　　evoke humanity – and tie it to us
we've learned how odd people can be.
The listener's soul is spread
immersed in a diversion
　　　　(relief and inspiration)
　　　　　　cherishing
　　　　cost-free empathy.
The individuals constituting the audience
　　　come from varied backgrounds
　　　　　isolated destinies.
Each tries to picture the figures
and the contingencies of the plot-turns.
The storyteller draws it out
　　the types and obstacles
but the listeners fill it with life,
　　transferring emotions and dreams
　　from their own experiences,

pride in their strengths,
shame in their failures and weaknesses,
traumas they need to compensate for.
Part of his skill is in selecting
 just the right mix of
 personalities desires dilemmas
 that will encourage their in-pour.

 the unruly course life runs
 It may know its riverbed
   but we don't

It is from this role/purpose that poetry arose
 though one day it would part company

 Figures and deeds
  that came to epitomize human aspirations
    and fate

 Games of death.
 what is battle
 but a game of death?
 What is anyone's life
 but a game with death?

"You start with youth's excited and not very realistic aspiration to art. Some vague notions of how it could be modernized and improved. Combined with a personal urge to cry the circumstances of your unknown life. That will eventually mature and grow into the higher ambition of a general representation of life, with the nebulous belief that you're helping to save humanity. There comes that period when you're desperate, praying that you will be given something important to say – anything - and the means to say it, that others will judge worthy. How poignant it is then to look back at your deformed and shrunken caricatures and realize all you've accomplished was to tarnish and desecrate every subject you attempted to render."
 - Eugene O'Neill
 from "The Last Letters of Eugene O'Neill"

 Ambition when young
 can't help but be romantic.

You hope to spin a captivating art
impressing the reading realm
with the texture and content
of life as we experience it. Magnified.
Accuracy that packs an impact,
revelatory dredges from the depths,
human feelings & motivations divulged,
written in your own indelible style,
pounding one insight after another
  (no slow plodding development here,
    all innovation, unbroken inspiration).
Your brilliance will be proclaimed,
you'll manufacture a persona to suit
which everyone, fawning, will buy.

Now it seems so ridiculous
a childish 'Look Mom what I did!',
vain from beginning to end.
yet that aspiration launched
      [the non-career]
  the study of the world and soul
in go-blind go-mad practice
  art by an unseen back road

    Having youth's tastes
     (for the 60's anyway)
      Surrealism
      rock's acts of rebellion and power
      drugs as an opening to the spiritual
      the search for secret truths
      alternative values
      bulwark against materialism
      Recognizing and rejecting the false
      resisting conformity and coercion
      Choosing the wild (in the human world)
      over timeclocked trained indoor work
    Though I now cringe at the naivete
    who would I be otherwise?

to establish yourself
   to be Authentic
the disadvantage of youth
people glance at you
and discount anything you have to say

                      I turn out to be, hypocritically,
                      the worst violator imaginable.
                      The same person who when young labeled
                      the carriers of society's common wisdom
                      brainless soulless drones - fools & tools;
                      now that he's old, starts with the prejudice
                      that anything any young person attempts
                      is certain to be empty worthless pretense.

How to get others to take you seriously?
that's why there was/is so much posturing
      clothes
      hair
      music
      tattoos
      piercings
      motorcycles
to stand apart – the pose as declaration
contempt for society's opinion,
'I know you for what you are.
Your opinion (of me) I spit back.'
That relationship the most important.
The role, defining hip, if successful,
means that you will be taken
as the ultimate insider (by outsiders).
Peer rivals have to be regarded
as the serious threats they are.
Should nothing work out
your fallback is prepared,
'Hey I never cared.
   Didn't you pick up on that?'

Concentrated experiences are
one way to appear 'for real' risking
as rockers and rappers formulate a heavy image
          language
          sex
          drugs
          guns
intensity push to ever more extreme
appear willing to throw it all away
Start hard   danger
Nothing's as impressive though
as dissatisfaction with success:
    'I'm so unhappy
      fame, money, makes no difference
        I dive into drugs
        I may not come up ...'
or: 'I come from the ghetto'
      unchallengeable background
        if it means playing a thug unto death
          - so be it.
Though usually mostly an act at first
finding you can't get out, stop
    Image demands
that catch when the expectations
create an environment that comes to get you.
A whirlpool not everyone survives.
You have to be big and brave in another way,
relenting to feel, to be real, not the pose,
 - to change and be willing to show it.

Underground Outsider.
The literary world is a little more subtle
    but not much.
When I was young the heroic counterculture figure
was the disaffected anti-hero loner
independently going his own way
    disdainful of all the small conventional minds
that swim in schools and decide winners

(a smart attitude, in case they don't pick you).
Eschewing both the corrupt elites
    patrons who made certain
    that the life in any art they 'owned'
    was safely boxed,
and the philistine masses
    (may the revolution forgive us)
    with their god-awful taste.
Acting as the terrifying prophet
     (in a stylish trench coat though)
The key was not to care
thus you alone could be objective
not influenced
not concerned with anticipated reactions.
a perfect zen indifference
the penetrating perception
the filing of a fearless report
in appropriately stark terms.

For every living man
there's a thousand dead.

Its natural for the unaligned
to be distant from what he observes
all part of his tragic aura
    the burden exuded in the style
An individual who won't be cowed or bribed
unbiased pilgrim, vagabond, traveler who can't stay
ultimately delivering the truth
description of our crisis circumstances
and our corrupt nature.
We, the dissenters, immediately recognize and accept,
enjoying that the judgment riles the phonies
with their stake in the popular fake.
It's striking though how the types looked to
    as contrast stand-ins for 'real'
are always the same untouchables at the bottom:
small time crooks, prostitutes, prisoners,

winos, drug addicts, and your full-bore nuts.
     society's victims
        those who've quit playing the game
For some reason we accept this too
(possibly as a byproduct of Christianity),
'ground' reality is there - with the downtrodden.
Undeniably there's something to this
  even if it brings distortion.

        And there's the ancient hazard
        you can't know the chambers
           of who you are
           and who others are
        without descending down into them.
        But down there you run the risk of capture,
        of getting beguiled
        by the power and fluency of the negative.
           It can take over your personality
              without noticing it your whole mind
                  your taste
                  your art.

When you finally incarnate as this disinterested observer
you're less conscious of the advantage of objectivity
   than of the disadvantage of not caring.
The only apparent benefit
is the immunity to criticism.
However this is depreciated by the fact
    that you no longer care what anyone says
         bad or good
         - possibly helpful advice.
The motive to write has been scrubbed off
    What is worth writing about?   Why?
    Who would I be writing for?   Why?
Writing itself is no longer taken
     to have some self-evident intrinsic value.
Even the previously unassailable presumption
that writing naturally possesses – or can possess

something inherently humane and worthwhile
    is eyed with suspicion
When all purposes and perspectives seem rife with egoism,
when writer's thoughts and readers' seriousness look absurd,
    more than the dross of personality has been lost.
If one is disdainful of all mediums, old as well as new,
    of all citizens and all editors,
who is able to give you that pep talk or upbraid
on the importance of any work or any deadline?
Why should you not procrastinate till the end of time?
It comes as a surprise that indifference
turns out not to be perfectly neutral.
It has a perspective. It has a flavor.

Yes ambition merges with the commercial,
    compromise downward, flatter, feed,
        entertain   occupy
exaggerate for maximum effect,
    do artificial, become artificial,
    swept away
    risk never returning.
But whole rejection as a course
    might be worse
    with no redeeming contribution.

After I turned 40
it was impossible to ignore
how perverse I had become.
Of the few I would let read my writing
my response was always exactly backwards.
    (I don't include 'salt of the earth' folk;
    their appreciation – always a surprise,
    always pleased, and made me happy.
    For some reason - to feel justified.)
Referring to those with literary comprehension,
if feedback was negative, that was quite alright.
Perplexity, even distaste – I was fine with that.
But an appreciative response bothered me.

I'd start wondering how I had failed.
Should they go further - penetrate and catch
   the intention and design,
     perceive what I had worked the hardest on,
I was sent into a self-doubting funk.
What exactly had happened to me?
How had my internal values gotten so twisted?
   I had been a kid who subscribed to
     - I think I still subscribe to -
      the old YMCA saw:
       'healthy spirit, mind, and body'.
How had I ended up so perverted?
Though I blame the authenticity mission
   there also must have been a collapse,
     a capitulation of character.

There is some irony, not to say justice,
that a course chosen in youth's heat and hurry,
mustered to repel doubts and prove yourself,
bequeaths a trajectory the older self
now recognizes as too limited,
but lacks the skills or energy to alter.

        When young
        aided by what you don't know
        about yourself and the world,
        believing in effects you can produce,
        in your capability
        to improve and change
          (yourself and the world)
        you don't hesitate to initiate.
        When old you don't even start.
        Because that faith has been forfeited.

    You find the particular kind of intelligence
      you devoted so much time to develop
               and sharpen
   has become passé, unwanted.

Less for being out of step
   with contemporary fashion and taste
   so its quality gets overlooked,
more for its obscurity,
being an ability no longer appreciated,
no longer even visible or intelligible.

Meanwhile you realize that the ordinary guy
  a normal job   wife and children
probably living in the suburbs,
who will never know, even third hand,
all that you've reconnoitered,
is the one possessed
   of what is meaningful.
You might carry trace element residues
that could be detected/decoded
by some precision instruments
   (that don't yet exist)
that would prove your testimony true.
But for all of that you might as well be
   a surplus lab animal
after the experiment has been run.

Maybe we should rephrase all this,
turn it into a paradoxical aphorism:
   There is something worse
   than getting sucked into the game.
   Not getting sucked into the game.

with everything you learned
   where are the famous hard edges?
All those definitive truths
   (you set out to bag),
the ultimate nature of the world,
   essentials of the living.
Everything turns out to be flexible,
   soft, fuzzy and subjective.

And there's another paradox.
At the same time as all this work is being done
on the construction of a hard-shell agent actor
    (or is it actor agent?)
energy and attention must be diverted
to the development of a sensitivity
able to register the finest impressions.
Set to study people, moods, emotions,
nuances and hidden motives.
Exact language – every connotation;
so that whatever has to be described
can be accurately conveyed by wording
    with suggestive consonance.
These two programs are in such extreme conflict
what metaphorical dilemma could represent it?

    Is it the adventurer proudly returning,
    prepared to give an engaging stimulating travelogue,
    finding his hosts have commissioned a painting -
    an absurd Henri Rousseauean scene on a huge drop
    hanging directly behind him on the stage?
    No matter how often he directs the audience
    to look at the objects of his prosaic photographs,
    their attention is distracted by the vivid fantasy.

    Or is it the walking-dead cynic
    handed an extraordinary instrument,
    which due to his native talent,
    a favorable upbringing - proper training,
    he has the unique skill to play;
    yet has lost the motivation and spirit?

Quietly sitting to the side at a local gathering
enjoying all the different types,
I idly muse who here could get my poetry?
And the probable answer is no one.
(This doesn't bother me in the least, it amuses.)

Provided you could get them to read poetry
my glyphs would strike them as very strange.
They'd be wondering the whole time:
    'Why does Lund employ such peculiar terms
    and have so many awkward thoughts?
    Is this weird stuff popular with that set?'
It would serve as a grammatical Rorschach test.
Not that they wouldn't be polite to my face,
and even charitable privately in their assessment,
    'Considering how his brain is boiling,
      he manages remarkably well.'

> *People better than us*
> *but of course inferior*

They have their sit-coms.
      diversions   relaxations
They don't spend their days attentive
to the strains we hobbyists attempt to trace.
We say they're choosing the face of matter
    over all that's inside, all that's higher.
But without the confusion that comes with
    reflective reductive thought
they are real - in a way innocent,
never seduced by insubstantial abstractions
never pretending to be more
    or other – than they are.
After all animals are real.
Even if we could maintain
    - and its dubious -
  that our art does twine
    the double helix of beauty and truth
  it could be countered
    that all of it is incorporated
      in the world
        very much their world
    and in the drama of their lives.
  If they never encounter beauty and truth

    as extract examples
        or known and labeled entities
    So what?
  Those elements are contained within
    and maybe that's the natural way
    incorporated with everything else.
In this shift we are the ones
arguing on behalf of the artificial.
    They have burdens
  without intellectual emollients,
  let them have their escapes.
They're not searching for meanings,
their lives are too jammed with them already.

            Poetry is a way of speaking
            (thinking is a way of speaking)(to yourself)
            communicating – sensations
            including mixed emotions and complex ideas.
            Though none of my poetry
            is meant to be read aloud -
            there's only the slightest trace of anything aural,
                I want a lone reader
                in the silence of a sealed off room.

    I learned the hard way
    not to push beyond conscious control.
    Even if, as the maker, you're still recognizable,
    the results aren't expressive, they're clumsy blobs.
    In the end I rejected breaking up sense
       on aesthetic grounds,
    correct reasoning turned out to be
       perfectly beautiful.

                No one in this Godforsaken wasteland
                    knows what poetry is

  By some contorted but balancing justice
  the only ones who appreciate your art

are the ones who don't need it,
    the mandarins.
Gourmands all their lives
going from one delicacy to the next.

The dissident hip in the oppressing city
suppressed, inert and uninspired
staring at the gray dull everyday
   forever shut out
   forever kept in this relationship
a busy world that spurns them,
which they need - to reject back.
They shirk the hard work real art requires,
unprotected-protected (inadvertently)
by the grueling conditions of a world
their lifestyle sentences them to.
Dressing in antagonistic alienation.
Why poetry? (it could've been any art)
no plan
begun by retreating to an identification
not to be confused with -
and stay hipper than - the dopes.
drifted to this rich penury.
a black and white philosophy
which yields a life
            with black professed
            gray endured
            intoxication needed,
grievances and attitude
despair stoically balanced
as the crowd moves on
         the bus's exhaust

If I ever found any substance in the avant-garde
but I never did

Of course it wasn't the hip, rap or slammers,
or the mandarins,

the pathetic rhymmeter-re-verse conservatives,
nor the identity political-victim petitioners,
who killed poetry in America.
It was the academic slash critics.
The cleric specialists,
the priesthood in charge of its preservation
    deferred to
because their comprehension was presumed
    widest and deepest.
A fatal delusion.
As the dying dead always do
they made it about form, not essence.
    They need material examples
        to point to, write about, teach about;
            so the living representations of life,
                of flowing water, fire and air,
                were replaced by shards of baked clay.

    Poetry got entrusted to people
who didn't know its heart,
didn't know what it was.
Yet there's no doubting their devotion
behold them publicly prostrating
    at selected shrines
(too often the wrong ones).
Remember poets and academics
not only share didactic dispositions
they also share the same *quiet desperation*
    intellectual ennui.
When they don't 'do' anything
- which they pretty much can't -
time stalls   and stretches
    feels tortuous.
Their bathos appears ridiculous
to outsiders who only see
    an apparently easy occupation
    with plenty of free time and idleness.

But their torment is pressed by the feeling
that they should take advantage of the lull
    to do 'important' work
while they lack inspiration to do anything.
They are torpid, the atmosphere empty.
They are lovers who demand
a recreation of a moment now past,
when emotion gushed unexpectedly.
Dress in a certain way,
move and speak in a certain manner,
all to rouse a ghost feeling.
They know they'll have to justify this
but they're confident in their ability.
Contemporary works they like
will always have a resemblance
    in tone   mood   or shape
    to one of their sacred relics.

        if its fan love
        what is fan love?

Whether as critics or teachers
   or self-conscious poets,
they're always antiquarians, collectors.
They stand at the Museum entrance yelling,
   "No no no. That's not good enough.
   Look in here, you'll find true excellence."
Pointing back to their preserved specimens.
Pushing-closing the Monastery's heavy doors
keeping out the tampering air and colors
of the rampant world
   all of it a distraction
There is work – study – processing to be done.
Perversely words become idols
   more important than what they represent.
Like every priest of every religion
the desire for order becomes an obsession.
Life isn't neat

But here inside
   quiet and peaceful
      the writ never moves.
There's space for revelation, but it seldom arrives.
And its hard to recapture that initial inspiration
the rapture rarely visits
   each print diminished and dimmer
      the feeling growing fainter
   but its never admitted
     compensate
        force
     con yourself
        (and they do.)

                       The real holy book of God
                          is the entire World

   all things curve
   they don't continue straight.
   The test is never obvious or easy.
     I believe it has to get harder
       so those coming later, or last,
         don't have every advantage.
        That would be unfair.
   Hierarchy always prefers - trusts
        literal adherence
     authority and orthodoxy preserved
   but keeping artifacts infallible
       whether religious
            political
            scientific
            or artistic
   chutes a straight line
     and gets you stranded off in emptiness

   Their anointed make poetry seem irrelevant
      strategies too clever
       cocky wording puzzles & ciphers

    impossible to penetrate
        with their incestuous references
    unless you are in their sect. (The point.)
Even when they speak of 'voice'
        or 'language',
they don't mean a voice people can understand
        or the language we share.

                Still as late as it is
                there's a goodness in poetry that comes through
                Why else would so many prisoners seek it out?
                hungering for vitality – life and meaning
                they sense it can be here, packed tightly in;
                other views – emotions - lives.
                Of course now you need a machete to get to it.

Let us – arbitrarily – posit
    all that could have been
but didn't happen, as a half.
Its a half we can never see
blocked even from imagination
        by what is.
Unconsciously we disparage
the idea of unrealized alternatives
        as ephemeral and untenable
        not even a possibility.

                There are no artists in our time
                    only political figures

When you labor on something many drafts
and it turns out – for whatever reason
unsatisfactory - or not to fit
You're attached - its your baby.
You can't forget the prospect you imagined.
Then there's all the work you put into it.

    Let it go

This won't be a tragedy
it simply wasn't the time.
all of it issued from you
it will be easily reabsorbed.
When it reappears
in a new superior form
in a more opportune place,
at an angle that gently surprises
it will fit perfectly
where it truly belongs.
You'll recognize how right
it happened to turn out.

Nothing's ever lost.
I've seen this happen
I know it's true.

        As one put off - not trusting
        poetry cast in the overwrought
        When I turn to look at my own lines
        suffused with melodramatic urgency,
        as if a figure (it has to be me)
        pacing, without resolve, or any plan,
        along an old fortress wall
        built atop a cliff's edge,
        as in a dream
        aware of the risk only peripherally,
            but with an unreliable mind
            in a desperate state
            stuck in this climatic conundrum
            unable to figure it out.

        You can't control poetry
            One shouldn't try
        but I'm not in control of anything

        The fierce fight
        to keep free of any influence
           is successful
        but is the outcome civil?
        and if not
        haven't you forfeited the right -
        by not partaking of the common life,
        to speak or contribute anything?

        Repeatedly you presume it's ending
        only to find yourself still here
        the world still going on,
        a blink – your take on it all
        changes   a little   again.

    The enterprise has come down
      to something between you and God.
    Now that doesn't sound crazy does it?

Though the ambition when very young
was to rely on imagination
   put on a show
   go for impact, take readers on a trip;
contemplating context and set-up,
I think from the great novelists
came the appreciation of how crucial
was trust in the narrator's wisdom.
If the story's world made sense,
   character dynamics,
   key details,
impressed us as right,
we'd open ourselves up fully
to its emotional pith.
I was no longer satisfied then
with creating the appearance of knowing,
I wanted to know.
The would-be seeker
joined the would-be artist.

Plus there were mysterious interactions
on occasion with the spiritual dimension.
The path I found myself on
     diverted from the Eastern,
which, as I understand it anyway,
advises rising above the thinking-machine-mind.
I didn't do that. I entered the maddening maze.
The gamble assumed - if you survived
     and weren't hopelessly deluded,
that you'd learn to wield the pieces,
and should you reach the immutables,
presumably having started with ability
you'd be able to render
what you discovered intelligibly.
To be honest I wasn't prepared for how crudely
     the possession of language was proffered,
     almost physical, and like an exclusive claim.
I had thought of it as an important asset of course,
but not as some primary prerequisite.
Apparently this facility/faculty came first,
it had to be in your bones, in your being.
[If my route is a confusing example a better one
would be Providence picking Darwin over Wallace
     as the one to be identified with evolution
     because he was the better writer,
even though Wallace was closer to the truth.]
After language there was a whole sequence of rings.
You had to have inspiration.
Inspiration was essential in picking the right ideas.
The right ideas were essential in training the mind.
A trained mind essential for learning how to think,
which you needed to sort the data.
This data you'd need if you made it all the way
as they constitute (or at least are perceived as)
definitive and persuasive 'concrete fact' evidence,
able to put convincing flesh – body -
on what you purport to be the ultimate answers.
Language as common currency seemed to thrust

centering yourself in the midst of American usage.
Whether my dissociation is a desired objectivity,
or an extra (as in 'clinical') I will leave to others.

        The fact that I hated formal poetics
        didn't save my work from categorization.
        I never saw that my approach
        kept too much of the traditional
            the parts of our inheritance I loved.
        Naïve faith in my perceptions.
        Naïve faith in my ability to describe them.
        Naïve faith in readers' ability to understand.
        Everything about my aesthetic was passé,
            the current had moved on – long ago.
        Simply standing still as the tide withdrew
            I had became - was left - a reactionary.

    I've always been lost.
    but I have a hunch (hope?)
    that it might be a lost person
        who finds.

If I'm reading the ether right
a key in our time is 'cooperation'.
With my loner bent,
alienation that might be terminal,
this might seem like a stretch.
I do love people. I find them fascinating.
I subscribe to equality and cooperation,
I was raised by radicals,
with egalitarianism as a prime principle.
    And I learned later on my own
      that God is in all of us.

        Don't we know its true that there are moments
            (all of time constituted of moments)
        when certain artists and works
        fortuitously embody the zeitgeist.

Their strengths, qualities, the combination
    takes – propels them to fame.
They feel and ride the swelling magnification
and simultaneously discover self-confidence.
(Isn't this like, or maybe the same as,
being surrounded by new people,
feeling infused with a liberated power
that has a rightness to it
    a 'coming into your own'
linked to the fact that they don't know you.
Whereas those who do know you confine
    fix and reduce your range
    by that very knowledge.)
These artists - or their celebrated creations,
may subsequently appear only a fashion
that after a short season are discarded
and when recalled, or seen in storage,
evoke embarrassment, nostalgia, or sadness.
Others though, once they join, never leave.
Regarded as indispensable,
a permanent prominent presence.

    Poets can speak for the dead
       for mountains
           rivers
           trees
           animals
           birds
           clouds
           the land
           rocks
           the ocean
           the Sun
           a people
           an age
           an experience, a memory
           a house

                pieces of furniture
                old watches, scrolls, novelties & toys
                anything you like.

        What if all art is imbued
        with the spirit of the artist?
        depending, even after completion
        on a quality of the soul
            breathed into it
                by its creator.

    When our slow world is dry earth
    poetry can be flowing and wet.
    When our days are tiresome
    it can be a song that brightens,
    that recalls us to joy and goodness.

When we think of what could have gone into
    forming the idea of the poetic
from chance phrasing that pleased so much
    it was isolated and examined,
to patterns, rhythms of sound
    that worked to enrapt.

The shaman's chant and spell
    into the trance state
lent poetry that cadence and slant
and bequeathed the reception
    of attentive awe, reverence.

Pithy folk sayings taught condensation.
The importance of recognizing -
and emphasizing - what was key.
The selection of the right word and phrase.
The composition, to create the effect desired.

            The contribution of individuals
            from life-at-stake experiences,

confronting one of the great elementals:
  the immense Ocean, limitless, all-powerful.
the thick Forest, denying sight, fear ruling the night.
  the vast Desert, no water, struggle to keep going,
    to think, even to breathe.
Before entering these a person couldn't help but feel
  their small size,
    that they were 'at the mercy of'.
It would have been natural to talk to yourself.
It would have been natural to address a plea-prayer
  to that great entity   to spare you.
Since the danger and fear would have squeezed
  any person to fullest alert,
its not surprising if survivors
had everything engraved in their memory,
the hinged emotions
their thought: word for word.

        Of course causes of concentration
        can occur in the everyday also.
        For self, for loved ones.
        The 'struggle to exist'
        disease possessing - outcome unknown.
            Women had childbirth.
            Men had combat.
            Everyone had death.

    Before the collection and order of civilization
    each individual would have been alone
    to make of their dreams what they could.
    Intriguing but probably also disturbing.
    These strange internal alternative realities,
    with an assaultive wildness,
    yet also under some unseen constraint.
    Familiar and strange, everything mixed up.
    The unreal actors and action felt compelling.
    Dreams, the range of our private imagination,
        first taught symbolizing.

Only in modernity, after mass print production
pressed readers with an overabundance
did we lose our natural response to the word.
Earlier, from outside, people still saw the magic,
    the divine gift in the 'word'.
(Most modern people are unable to apprehend
what the Platonist meant at the beginning of John.)
Presumably, in an even earlier epoch,
there would have been a similar appreciation
at the miracle of the spoken word.
Only wide-eyed children now
    learning to speak
    learning to read
perceive the wonder of these manifestations
- how ingenious their invention and operation.
Too soon this response will dissipate
as well-meaning adults command their attention,
guiding them towards endless problem-solving
with promised breaks for the recreational.

        I wonder if our ancestors were superior to us,
        minds more trusting of intuition,
        more accepting of the world-as-presented
        knowing that there's a mystery in everything
            and some processes can never be resolved?
        Or were they, it being human nature, just like us,
        cobbling something plausible together,
            letting it serve in the meanwhile,
        and over time the placeholder, just being there,
        gets accepted, assumed to be the obvious answer.
        Until the day its overturned.
        Either by a startling new discovery's evidence,
        or a slow erosion evolution which takes away
            all its surrounding support,
        leaving it to appear as archaic and absurd as it is,
        its replacement then causing only a shrug.

All of this history – our inheritance
has gone into our present understanding
of poetry in a purer way
as a distillation concentration
    of the spirit

to act from fear
is not faith

sudden seasons

What if in the beginning
the sun and moon
had been given opposite assignments?
The Moon had been charged with
      heat and light
         life
and the Sun had been
   the mere attending mirror
      flat
colorless reflected illumination.

With the Moon
as the chariot of our days
  everything skipping all about
    unreeling - more emotional -
following her skittish whims.

The variation would affect perception
and our moods::
  "You appear angry. Are you angry?"
  "No. Well yes - Yes I am!"
and realizations:
  in just the right light
  suddenly you see
    You do love a certain person.

[Who would be in charge of the tides?]

We'd pass through all the seasons
   every month.
Waxing crescent   a brief spring.
Waning crescent   a quick fall.
Days around the full Moon
  constituting a week of summer.
You could never pack clothes away.

Winters would be more severe,
   but they wouldn't be as dark.
As the Sun, being the Sun,
   would stay reliable,
outside that reflected cool colorless light
during the time that used to be day.
Sunrise and sunset would lose
the dramatic effect they once had for us,
but one could depend
that in the duration in between
     the Sun
would always have its ghost light on
     always full
to help people see their way.

Since visits by the Moon are irregular
they wouldn't be taken for granted.
At dawnbreak   the growing warmth
 and rainbow-light
parents yell to wake children
    "Moon! Get outside!"
In more advanced countries
  (except for agriculture)
no work would be allowed
- the time reserved for 'living'.

Every month a May Day
    Flowers!
And an Easter.
  Thanksgiving
  Christmas.

No more droughts.
Yet floods would quickly dry.
There would be innumerable enclosed farms
with rollaway roofs.
Maybe all buildings
would have gardens on top.

Skiing one week.
Planting the next.
Then sunning and surfing at the beach.
On to harvest.

Nature would adapt.
Every month trees would leaf out
                    and shed.
Fruit would flower, bud, ripen.
Crop plants would burst in growth,
or be so hardy they could survive the cold.

Insects would probably go through
their whole life cycle every month.
Animals, birds, plants,
   would have to evolve differently
but we have that capability within us.
We've probably been coddled
    since the dinosaurs.
And after all
there would have been millions of years
to adjust to this different schedule.
We shouldn't expect longevity though.
Animals might live half as long.
Even humans – 40 would probably be it.
We'd be exhausted.
Character would be altered also.
The young forced to get wise prematurely,
adults kept childlike by all the changes.
Those who weren't 'moon moody'
   would probably be stoic.
People would have increased appreciation,
energy and enthusiasm - ready to leap.
Until the day when the spent body
   couldn't move.

MY DAD

You must know how much I loved you

If I had known
    it was the end
I wouldn't have jerked you up like that
       so violently
clapped you on the back.
I was so exhausted by then
through lack of sleep
you had been having trouble breathing

Your head fell all the way over to the side
which makes me cry to think of it

I just would have hugged you
    held you
told you how much I loved you
how much I'd loved you my whole life
  I was worn out
     fatigued
  out of my head

If I had known it was the passing
     I would have left you in peace   to sleep
        covered you with some sort of prayer

              "You know I loved you Dad.
               All my life I loved you."

My father can never be dead

                    *

                  I know you loved your father
                     but I loved you more

John Lund remains unknown
   Dad was never forthcoming about him
even though out front about the alcoholism.
John started working at 14
and he also started drinking.
He drank a quart of whiskey every day of his life.
Dad would quickly add
   he was always a great worker -
could do anything - any job that needed being done.
Old photograph, with his fanatic John Brown eyes,
the obvious source of the terrifying Lund will.
Dad never filled in his whole character.
The world was farms - small town Iowa
Norwegian spoken in the home
8th grade educations
There had to have been something eating him.
Later his father would offer him farms – land
   he would spurn it all.
Two brothers enlisted in WW I
   both got mustard-gassed,
   both received 'Dear John' letters
     (one quit women for good),
to John they were saps
getting conned by the propaganda.
In contrast to his wife, my grandmother,
who was a devout Lutheran,
John didn't attend church.
Which was quite remarkable in that community.

When my brother and I were small
Dad would tell us tales about his father
in which he was the hero
   a very tough hero.
Dad said he could learn any language,
   play any instrument.

He hated to see animals mistreated.
He had been a mule-skinner at one point

      and maintained you got better results
with kindness and simply speaking encouragingly
    to the mule or horse.
If he saw someone using a whip he'd grab it from them
threatening if he ever caught them doing it again
    he would use it on them.
On the other hand he had a series of German shepherds
all of whom he called 'Shep', considered work animals,
    and never allowed to enter the house.
Traps covered a wall
sometimes Dad would wake on winter mornings
to see all the traps gone
    and his father's tracks in the snow.

In one story John was working as a brakeman.
He'd fallen asleep (probably sleeping one off),
when two railroad dicks came upon him,
not realizing he worked for the railroad,
    judging him to be just another hobo,
they picked him up and were carrying him to a ledge
where they intended to toss him.
John awoke, saw what was in progress, and said,
"Boys, we're going to have to make a decision."
From the authority of his voice
and the strength coursing through his limbs
they knew if anyone was going to be flying into space
    it would be the two of them.
They put him down and apologized.

Besides volunteering his father's alcoholism,
another peculiarity was Dad's blunt explanation
of how the Lunds came to be the marshals.
He said it had nothing to do with virtue,
everyone in the county knew them,
and knew no sane person would cross them.
You'd have thought it an opportunity to boast
of respect and a reputation for integrity,
but Dad was too honest, and he knew the truth.

One time as a boy a neighbor's dog bit Dad.
John went over and told the man
if this ever happens again
    first I'll shoot the dog
    then I'll shoot you.
The fellow knew this wasn't angry bluster.

Dad always said in the ring no one could beat Joe Louis,
but in a barroom brawl no one, including Joe Louis,
could take John Lund.
It's a very odd thing for a law-abiding man
to tell his two law-abiding sons,
but as a child it was peculiarly curious and impressive.

We lived in South Central LA.
When White flight rolled through the area,
our parents, radicals, in the vanguard for equal rights,
refused, on principle, to move, even though we just rented.
Naturally then one of our favorite grandpa tales
concerned the time he came upon three guys
beating up a Black man.
He told them you're going to fight him one at a time,
or you're going to have to fight me too.
They knew what that meant,
and they were unwilling to fight one on one, so they left.
So the only time we made a trip to San Diego to visit him
it was a shock to hear Grandpa call his black dog Nigger.
We couldn't comprehend how this could be.
Dad tried to get his father off out of earshot,
pleading with him not to use that name.
They were close enough that we could still hear them.
The old man couldn't understand.
He kept protesting that the dog was black,
as if that made the name natural, almost inevitable.
(He was proud of how many cats this dog had killed.)
Dad, no doubt feeling trapped,
then huddled with us and tried to explain

how difficult it was for an older person
to change how they had always thought about things,
to accept that the world had moved on.
But for my brother and myself
our problem was how to reconcile
here - in the flesh - the hero of the tale
   unsung champion of tolerance
   defender of the persecuted
calling his dog this heinous name.
Children presume every person's character
   to be one solid substance
the good are good, the bad are bad,
    all the way through
they are not prepared for contradictory complexities,
   that a person prompted to act
   out of a basic sense of fairness,
   could also be prone to the prevalent prejudice.
The stories about Grandpa stopped.

                Have you noticed how often ordinary people
                   don't follow the expected/accepted
                      but veer to an unruly choice?
              That among those we've known when faced
              with a certain odd 'situational' circumstance,
              they decide on a very idiosyncratic course
                that makes sense to them,
              and not care a fig that they're violating
                standard societal norms.
              Peter Lund, father of all the tough sons,
                was an easy going fellow.
              Lars Jondal on the other hand
                (father of my grandmother Helen)
              according to Dad, was a strict patriarch.
              No one touched their food until he did.
              Dad, the only grandson, was the exception.

Decades later Dad, sitting out on the deck
sipping beers, loosened and ruminating,

conceded - pushed out - that when entertaining
   in breaks from playing music,
John would tell groups humorous stories,
and a surefire favorite
was Rastus in the chicken coop,
featuring the stereotypical shiftless stupid Black.
   Farmer hears a racket, comes out with a gun,
      yells, "Who's in there?"
   Rastus, in a shaky voice, answers back,
         "Nobody but us chickens."
   Always good for a laugh.

   Grandma could hold her own as a worker.
   She could hitch a team of horses by herself.
   Was a whirlwind at cleaning, sewing, cooking.
   Whipping out delicious pies in no time.
      During the Depression
      She'd send Dad out with a fresh pie
      asking - depending on the size –
         for a quarter or 50 cents.
      There were always buyers.
   She was the disciplinarian,
         his father only hit him once
         - a 2 by 4 on the butt -
         when he snuck out on a harvest moon.
   Dad was an only child
   but if he was being cheeky he had to make sure
   that he was out of her range.
   He said she slapped so hard your head rang.
   There's no getting around the fact though
   even when I knew her grandma could nag.
   She'd get on John, and she'd stay on him.
   He'd never touch her, but he might break
      every piece of furniture in the house.

            Two pets should be mentioned.
            Possibly Dad's favorite was a little pig.
            He said people don't appreciate how smart pigs are.

    He treated it like a dog and it behaved like a dog.
    Unfortunately little pigs grow up into hogs
    and can't be pets anymore so it had to end sadly.
    When Dad was little the family had a rat terrier,
    and he swore by its intelligence too.
    He said the dog saved him twice.
    As a toddler he'd climbed into the hog pen,
      the dog jumped in after him,
    barking and snarling, he kept the hogs at bay
    until Dad could be rescued
      (John blamed Helen for this).
    Another time Dad wandered into the corn fields
      which in Iowa are as vast as the seas,
    and that clever dog kept running in circles
      around him - shaking the stalks,
    thereby showing the family where to look.

With John and Helen
the differences went beyond religion,
to his practices - like horse-trading,
which she couldn't approve of.
The biggest problem must have come
from the central role drink played in his life
the influence it had on all his behavior.

        Argument in the car
        probably after demanding John stop
          and he doesn't
        she jumps while it's still moving
          loses all her teeth.
        John blames Dad (still a kid)
         'You should have caught her.'

When he's 11 they move to San Diego
   soon are divorced.
As much as he loved his father
he never forgave him for suggesting
that he could come and live with him.

To even contemplate abandoning one's mother
to Dad violated both nature and morality.
And I don't think John ever gave her a red cent.
Dad lived with her until he married Mom,
and whatever job he had:
grocery store, construction, recreation,
National Guard, aircraft manufacture,
a good portion of his salary went to her.
When he went off to war, as his dependent,
most of his pay he had mailed to her.

Except for coming from small farm town Iowa
and being Norwegian they had nothing in common.
Later, in L.A., Grandma worked for a spell
as a domestic for some middleclass family
   that paid her peanuts.
She'd talk about them like they were royalty,
   they were so high - too kind - too generous.
Whereas John Lund, who stayed in San Diego,
prospered as an independent gardener,
pleasing his wealthy clientele with his ability
   to maintain their plants and grounds.
Yet he regarded them with bemused contempt.
He did all his tasks to perfection
not to ingratiate himself to a group of rich fools
but because that was the object of work -
   to strive for and achieve excellence.

Dad inherited traits from both.
He had a funny quirk in his enthusiasm for a new job.
At first the boss would be the greatest guy;
incredibly knowledgeable of what was pertinent,
astute, knowing when and how to react
   - deftly doing exactly what was called for.
On top of everything he was friendly and helpful,
   just a wonderful human being.
So modest, considering his knowledge and ability.
Almost invariably, as the job wore on,

    its allotted time closer to expiration,
the assessment of the poor fellow
    would have plummeted several levels.
Disappointments accumulated, familiarity with faults,
he would become, along with the job, barely tolerable.
Now, as the work was less challenging and important,
      the boss was no longer dynamic,
        usually shrinking to a pathetic figure.
There were notable exceptions though
    Art Sears at the Wilshire Y,
    Mr. Tynson at Juvenile Hall,
    Sol Oziel, at Van Nuys Probation;
    men who never faltered in his esteem.
And to be fair there had to be a whole host
of bosses and supervisors now lost in memory's foliage
who okayed and backed innovative projects and programs.
New places for YMCA summer buses to visit.
Roller skates for Juvenile Hall.
Rewarding good behavior at a youth detention camp
    with a trip to the beach.
The construction of a shuffleboard court
just for seniors at a huge park in Sherman Oaks.
Everywhere the introduction of new sports and games.
Dad was always older than other subordinates,
    with deeper and broader experiences,
which played a part in how his ideas were received.
Undoubtedly his enthusiasm helped too.
Yet in hindsight I think we're obliged to concede
that a lot of people in authority
must have been looking for ways to engage.

Mom never argued about a particular job
- Dad always had a surfeit of specific complaints -
but overall she wasn't happy with the ceaseless change
the restlessness and endless successions.
        the unsettledness

Dad wanted to make a difference
and there was a lot in society that needed remedying.
But after he instituted his innovations
with the whole world outside going on
the position would appear less consequential,
his duties too rote, the place too out of the way.

We weren't allowed to trick or treat —safety fears.
And we were the only kids in the neighborhood
who weren't allowed to play in the street.
It was funny that Dad, farm child – tractors, rifles;
    San Diego kid running wild;
young man 'hopping freights' to see the country;
    should turn out to be so safety obsessed.
One Halloween,
Mom and our sister went off somewhere together,
my brother and I were left alone with Dad.
I've forgotten the specifics
but we were upset, a promise or expectation dashed,
Dad in his stern coach/sergeant mode,
slamming it shut, not abiding any nonsense.
    (A parent's discipline is for the child's good
       - so they don't end up spoiled,
    but enforcement seems to coincide
    with having endured a bad day elsewhere.)
We recoiled in sullen sulks.
After awhile though I could see his mood had softened.
He had been reflecting
my boys are going to have a disappointing Halloween
What can I do – how can I change that?
He made overtures, suggested different things
    a board game   hot chocolate
all of which, maintaining our pout, we snubbed.
I had to stay in solidarity with my brother
but I was no longer feeling aggrieved. I was touched.
It was one of those moments
when you've been moving in a committed direction
then suddenly, emotion swung by a glimpse

you're traveling in the opposite direction.
As the expression goes
    my 'heart went out' to Dad.
We were continuing to act hurt
while he was the one really feeling
        remorse

        There are endearments only the poor know

I would occasionally have mystical experiences
overcoming me
   a sensing of the Oneness
   that extra-intelligence intelligence
I had no idea what was going on
it seemed every thing – everything -
   was getting absorbed.
It was all very spooky.
My parents valued the moral teachings of all religions,
but dismissed the more spiritual aspects as outdated
   residue from superstition-laded origins.
Since I saw my parents, an embattled minority,
   as absolutely right in their convictions
   absolutely right in how they perceived things
and subscribed to everything they did,
that meant the 'rational' was it.
Only material substances existed.
So I had no means of understanding what was going on,
let alone putting into words these strange experiences.
One night it was really strong.
Mom was away, probably at a political meeting,
   younger brother and sister already asleep.
I started to panic, feeling under assault and lost.
Not wanting to but with no other option
I walked to their bedroom
and asked Dad if I could come into bed with him.
I was far too old for this -
it would have been well within his role to say no.
Yet he didn't even question me,

maybe he saw how frightened I looked and sounded.
He had the AM station on that played classical music.

As an adolescent Dad would tell his mother
he was spending the night with his father,
and tell his father he was remaining home.
This way he was free to roam the city at night.
San Diego wasn't big then, but it was a Navy town.
He must have gone a little off the tracks
because later when he told his father
he had applied for a job
associated with the Sheriff's department,
John's caustic reply was, "They hire hoods now?"

What saved Dad more than anything else was
     sports   athletics
        the playground
He was a natural psychologist,
truly one of the best I've ever encountered
   at reading people thoroughly.
He seemed to have gathered a lot of his insights
from competitive team sports
tracking your own thoughts and emotions,
while perceiving how different types react
to the vagaries of a game
    their abilities
    whether they kid themselves
    or are honest.
    Is it all self
    or the team?
    How they react at a critical juncture
    when the pressure's really on.
    How success and flattery can ruin.
    How failure can motivate,
    engender the hard work that improves.
The importance of discipline, training, conditioning.
A coach told him cigarettes would limit stamina
and he quit.

                         He was a skinny kid with glasses
                         but one whose father
                         had him digging ditches as a child.
                         His looks were deceiving
                         and they masked that Lund fury.
                         He was quick, agile,
                              tough and determined.

Another kid on the playground
a little younger, was Ted Williams.
Everyone saw him as a future baseball star.
Dad said the playground director, Rod Luscomb,
was the one who taught him how to 'wrist hit',
and that was key to his power.
Dad maintained that most of the hitting stats
would have belonged to Williams
except as a fighter pilot
he missed 3 seasons in World War II,
and 2 because of Korea.

Dad was a four sport letterman,
with a sweater that proved it,
though he never wore it -
that would be too much like boasting -
though his mother proudly hung it in her closet.
He quit the baseball team at Hoover High
in support of his friend McCabe.
McCabe, like Dad, did things his own way.
They both thought the coach was playing favorites,
starting an inferior athlete as catcher.
(I have to add though that this other kid,
Ray Boone, had a long career in the majors.)

The exceptional football players from Hoover
made up the nucleus
of a great freshman football team at San Diego
- destined to go undefeated -

with not a few taken by USC,
a national 'powerhouse' back then.
Dad played one end,
all the other ends rotated on the other side,
he never came out of a game.
Not counting the first half of the first game,
when he refused to let them tape his legs
    (I don't know why)
The coach had declared no one plays who isn't taped.
Of course the coach was the one to give in.
Throwing the football in those days was rare,
it was mostly blocking and running.
Teams soon learned not to try Dad's side.
One heroic act – blocking a kick
- this before helmets came with facemasks -
had the kicker's cleats ripped into his mouth,
    brought all pride and glory to an end.
On the sideline they sewed up his bottom lip
and sent him back into the game.
The next day his teeth started raining out.
For a young man who took care in his appearance
    as well as his fitness
this was a devastating blow.
The school paid for a top dentist to make dentures,
    still he felt betrayed.
Probably sewing him up, sending him back in,
    stamped a sense of being used.
He walked away from the team
and away from the school
    without officially withdrawing.
Decades later when he went back to college
    to pursue a degree in sociology
all those F's came back up
and he had to work to balance them out.

When the war broke out he had a double deferment,
    as an only son, his mother as his dependent,
and as someone overseeing production

for an aircraft manufacturer.
Still he volunteered.
Certain with all his years in the National Guard
and the Coast Artillery, they'd place him in artillery.
Instead, because he had worked at Corvair,
and could type 70 words per minute,
they placed him in Operations
inside the new Army Air Force.
After training, he was sent to England.

Dad loved everything about England
    and everything about the English.
On his days off he wouldn't get drunk,
he'd travel to see different cultural landmarks.
He was slightly older than most of the 'Yanks',
was spared their brash embarrassing arrogance.
He respected the 'Tommies' as tough fighters
who had been fighting hard long before we showed up.
That said he didn't respect their bombers -
he wouldn't ride in a Lancaster even to sight see;
he said the Brits were included on missions for show.
Dad was very loyal to his unit's bomb crews,
he hated the horrific casualties they were taking.
He blamed Churchill and Eisenhower
for ordering low level daytime bombing.
As someone trained in artillery he knew this strategy
was serving them up to the German 8" cannons.
    (Ironically Mom, the real Party person,
        would end up voting for Ike - for Korean peace.)
One thing he could do, being in Operations,
was search flight records, see who was owed back pay.
He'd fill out the paperwork and request prompt action.
Many guys acted surprised to finally receive anything,
    and they'd offer Dad a cut for getting it.
He'd tell them: "This has nothing to do with me.
This is what you earned and were owed."

He found out a buddy from San Diego
had also been stationed in Britain.
At first he was delighted they could get together
but his old friend carried on obliviously,
mocking the Air Force as Hollywood glamour,
   glorified puffed up nonsense,
to Dad, who had witnessed whole crews,
guys he knew and liked, disappear, this was insulting.
Then he bragged of his success with English wives
   whose husbands were away fighting.
That was the end of that friendship.

After the war his ambition was to be a labor lawyer.
With help from the G.I. bill he went to a law school,
was only 6 units shy of graduating with a law degree,
when the State Board summoned him
to appear before them in San Francisco.
This was unprecedented for someone
who hadn't even taken the bar yet.
   He refused
and gave up the labor lawyer dream.
(Everyone else in the study group he led
   passed the bar exam.)

               Among Dad's political friends
               Carl Calendar was like a professor-mentor,
               Tracy, kind of a hothead, married a Japanese girl,
               who, along with her family, got interned.
               One friend didn't survive the Pacific war.
               Unable to get over malaria,
               Dad said they knew his politics,
                 so instead of shipping him home to recover
                 they repeatedly sent him back into battle
                    until he got slain.
               His best friend McCabe however wasn't political.
               He went along with handing out leaflets, stenciling,
               putting up posters, just out of friendship.
               Dad and McCabe became serious boxers.

McCabe was the best amateur heavyweight
in San Diego, while Dad was only a middleweight.
Sparring the only way Dad could take him
    was to exploit his temper.
McCabe didn't like it when his nose got hit
so Dad would keep jabbing at it until he exploded.
Then he could outbox him.
Dad had a bad left eye and he said it saved him.
The fear of one wrong hit to the good eye
    leaving him blind
stopped him from pursuing prize fighting
thus escaping the fate of ending up punch-drunk.
One day the pair visited John Lund's house.
Apparently McCabe was in a boisterous
    obstreperous mood.
John Lund lifted him off the floor
with one hand saying,
    "Son, you've got to settle down."
John Lund the mystery.
There weren't two men on earth
    who could take him
yet he drove around town
with a loaded 38 on the floorboard.
The disintegration of their little family of three
must have disturbed Dad
    but what ate at John Lund?
Marrying, moving to LA,
Dad lost touch with McCabe.
He came from money, and ended up a gambler.

Mom's explanation on leaving the Communist Party,
that they did a lot of talking, not much else,
and had failed at converting others to the cause,
   "We were among the youngest people when we joined,
   and we were among the youngest when we quit."
She had enlisted a month before Pearl Harbor,
   but Dad never really did join.
He believed in all the socialist ideals,

but he noticed that with all their talk about 'workers',
none of the people calling the shots were workers.

The FBI kept trying to get him to talk
    which was absurd.
He had always taught us to loathe rats, and
    "There's nothing lower than a stool pigeon."
Besides that Mom and Dad still loved
a lot of the diehards back in the Party,
including one of Mom's younger sisters.
    Whatever their utopian intellectual delusions
    they were dedicated to the greater good.
In our all Black neighborhood
we'd have two White FBI agents in suits
sitting in a car out front
pretending to read a newspaper.
Dad's legal studies helped him here,
when they'd be at the door requesting an interview
he'd courteously reply "I'd love to talk to you,
just let me see your warrant."

They got their revenge though.
Periodically catching up to where he was working
going up to the employer and insinuating
"You know who you have working for you?..."
One job after another.
There were some stand up guys,
like one contractor who said
"If you've got something to arrest him for -
arrest him. Otherwise beat it."
But most knuckled under. Didn't want trouble.
Even the head of the Burbank Y
(a guy I'd looked up to as a kid. A white rag.
Who I personally owed for picking me
    at the huge summer camp they owned
for one of the greatest experiences I ever had.
Letting the horses out in the early morning,
leading them to their water.

I would hop on a small white horse
    and ride bareback.)
He told Dad he'd give him a reference,
but only one over the phone, nothing on paper.

When Dad was in his 80's
we got a freedom of information notification
    reviewing the records…possible violation…
    there could be grounds for a lawsuit… et cetera…
    sign here to request copies of relevant documents.
I was curious, but he wanted nothing to do with it.
He considered all of it contamination.

He always loved children
and because of the emotional twist
his parent's divorce caused him,
his own experience was a motivation
to help troubled kids .
He understood how a disrupted home
could turn everything bitter,
    make the world seem cold.
And once rejection became your attitude
it was hard to pull away from it
  and get back to positive
      which requires effort   work.
Suspicion towards a hostile environment
          hopelessness
the wrong values and your old friends
still dwelling in that negativity -
a gravity pulling you back to bad habits.
His was a tough love approach.
You sent the message that you cared,
that you believed they could change;
but it was on them to make the commitment
  to dare those first hard steps
  and then keep on the constructive.

One of his best experiences was a pilot program
created for kids who fell into a no man's zone.
The schools had given up on them, didn't want them,
but their transgressions were short of Youth Authority.
Dad and another probation officer headed it.
Dave Eagleton was a saint. His philosophy was
this wonderful "Everyone's doing the best they can."
There was no behavior he couldn't understand and forgive.
Even after a boy physically attacked him
he questioned and lamented Dad's response
of kicking the kid out, sending him to prison.
The program had its own bus driver, and teacher.
(Dad regretted getting rid of one teacher solely because
he had categorized him as a Christian true believer.
He feared the guy might proselytize the kids.
In hindsight he thought his prejudice had cost them
the best man they ever had in that position.)
It was a stipulation that families had to participate.
Dad was deeply impressed at the percentage
of these kids who lacked fathers.
The father might show up every couple of weeks
     drunk   only to beat them up
but for most of them he was a phantom.

Dad ended his probation work in Van Nuys,
with adults, and it was a grind.
The accused and convicted protested innocence
even though they had a long sheet of priors.
The judges followed his recommendations.
Dad called jail "reality therapy".
He thought if he had stayed with Recreation
he could have played a more beneficial role,
    saving kids before they went bad.
With adults he was getting them too late.

To the old left's disgrace quite a few men
    were the worst sort of pigs and cads.
Dad in contrast always backed women's rights,

and supported Mom as she battled
    discrimination in employment.
Still in the early days of their marriage
I can remember him repeating that old cliché:
    "I wear the pants in this family."
That stopped after awhile.
When Dad would go back to college
to meet county requirements for the next level,
it seemed a good deal of the family income
came from Mom's steady drafting work.

Though few could rival his righteous passion
when a cause was just, he wasn't narrow.
One time the union leaders at L.A. Drug
wanted to go on strike simply to go on strike,
it was Dad who demurred,
    'They're not our enemies.
      We want them to be successful.'
When my brother and I were young
    and zealous,
little boys enjoying a picket line as if play
Dad hit us with a remarkable insight,
"Remember if we owned the factory
we'd be worse SOBs than that fellow."
Reminding us that it wasn't a case
of inherent goodness fighting inherent evil,
it was the position each person found themselves in
    the role – their circumstances
that determined how they viewed things.

He had a lot of wise sayings
like 'misery loves company'
and 'the worst slave driver is the ex-slave'.

                    There's something misleading
                      in this listing of virtues.
                    Not that they aren't true
                      but it suggests – implies

that love comes from worthiness.
I don't believe that.
I look around. I was lucky,
   my father was admirable.
But that wasn't why I loved him.
Love isn't confined to those
   with sterling qualities
I loved him because he was himself.
That person.
Children with parents
hamstrung with faults,
who disappoint again and again
   still love them.
And those parents, with faults,
   love their children.
Love is mysterious
a mix of magnetic attractive powers
   and complex qualities
   able to overwhelm flaws.

Frequently in aging the speed of decline
for mind and body separate,
one faltering much faster than the other.
A still strong mind
finds itself imprisoned in a weak body.
Or a still strong body loses its pilot.
But with Dad they declined together,
as his body broke down, strength and spine,
so did his short term memory.

A family visit, we all go for a stroll
on the side of the main drag.
I look at Dad, who's really enjoying
the walk - seeing the town again,
but with no self-awareness
he's walking like an R Crumb comic figure
legs exaggeratedly in front of his trunk.
I couldn't walk like that if I tried.

My independent and decisive father
had become a caricature.
I wasn't as embarrassed for myself
as I was for his real self,
a strong proud man
misrepresenting himself
   in this clownish manner.

Aging humbles many

   That form is still there
     and he is still there
       in there
   but now vulnerable

   One can adapt
   become fond of this new character
     establish a different relationship
       weight of daily interchange
        - his physical dependence -
     yet it's a violation of the prime bond
     because this person isn't them whole.

It seems wrong to even speak of Dad this way
he was always such a participant
   (in sharp contrast to this son
   an observer trying to figure things out).
In that way, and others, his other son
   is more like him - a participant.
But this portrait wouldn't be accurate
if I didn't include the final decline

     As the years had accumulated
     Dad had withdrawn more and more
       into his own world
     Though always very social
     to the end loving and enjoying people,

but now getting to the afternoon beers
seemed the objective of the day.
In the warm months
   he'd sit out on the deck
      gaze up at
    the trees, birds, sky
      in reverie.
He'd also brood
a reliance on alcohol
not only for that first feeling good
but for an upsurge flush of emotions
    part of it escape
pursuing his own private thoughts
and memories – with no opposition.
It would be fair to say I think
   that he'd always had a private side,
      somewhat moody.
The euphoria with nature was brief
compared to the plunge into thought
    and memory.

Of course thanks to the beer
I learned some things about the past
I wouldn't have otherwise.
Only once did he ever tell me
about visiting jail
when his father was being held.
It was a heinous charge, like molestation,
that some malicious person cooked up
to get rid of this drunk once and for all.
Because the charge was so shameful
John refused to speak of it -
   even to refute it.
Dad told me that a guard at the jail
had praised him, only a really good son
would stand by his father in this situation.
Dad hadn't stayed close
at the end of his father's life

    so he was probably reassuring himself
        that he had been a good son.

                He got more fussy and prickly
                A man who had always prioritized children
                    a life of making games
                        and wooden toys for their enjoyment
                now had little time or patience for them.
                It's sad but the younger grandchildren
                would never share, never meet his true self.

I tried over the years
in what I thought were low-key ways,
not confrontational, not argumentative,
to suggest alternative spiritual views.
That our real being was a soul,
trapped in the mold that made us,
death was an escape
   to a world exponentially superior.
There was no such thing as hell.
God wasn't a person
      simply the holistic sum of all that was.
      One was free to discard religion
      but the Soul was a reality
      and Heaven was a reality.
Nothing I said ever penetrated an inch.
He sloughed it all off as it was spoken.
I think he was one of those people
who use the most hidebound versions
of religion and its most rigid practitioners
     to define it
all in order to more easily dismiss it.
Though he honored all religions
     - for their ethical teachings
he disbelieved anything spiritual,
saying it all arose from primitive man's
      fear of death.
All of it an expansion of superstition.

He was a hardcore atheist.
In World War II, in a transport airplane
over the waters beyond Iceland
they experienced engine trouble.
Told to line up with parachutes on,
they all knew in the frigid Atlantic
life would be minutes, rescue doubtful.
The man in front of Dad,
a professing Christian sort,
shit in his pants as they waited.
Dad said, "What are you scared of ?
You know where you're going."
The plane managed to stay aloft.
The guy never forgave Dad.
Understandably.

Despite his father's skeptical example,
at his mother's instigation
Dad started life as a good Lutheran kid,
winning awards for never missing Sunday school.
Though some things always bothered him -
the pastor in Iowa standing up in the pulpit
    and denouncing Catholics.
That didn't seem Christian to him.
After they moved to San Diego,
    after his parents divorced,
when he was 12, I think in the 8th grade,
he reasoned as follows:
    If God existed, He wouldn't let children suffer.
    Children suffer. Therefore God doesn't exist.

So I couldn't offer him the solace & consolation
of an afterlife, even though I believe in it.
He wouldn't even entertain the possibility.
Surprisingly to me even as his faculties weakened
this conviction remained adamant.

Some effects from his upbringing lingered.
To humor his mother and Aunt Myn
he would occasionally take us all to a service
at this prosperous church they favored in Wilshire,
"Our Savior's Lutheran" (Missouri Synod).
The people were very nice if proper,
the interior impressive – sunlight on wood,
the exhortations mostly for doing good.
On the drive home Dad would lead a discussion
on what the moral of the sermon had been.

Dad respected true Christians
and regarded Jesus's ministry
    as very good and very high.
When he worked for the Y.M.C.A.
    he never thought their ideals
    in any way contradicted his own.
Whenever Dad would say
– cutting the presumptuous down to size –
    "There's only been one perfect person",
that perfect person he had in mind was Jesus.

                          *

    Is that stooped frail old man
        humped over
            back almost horizontal
  slowly poking-feeling his way with his cane
        my father?

Where did you think 'crooked old men' came from?
Everyone was spry and young once.

        I won't let you go.

    good health allows you to postpone reckoning.
        then deterioration
            impossible to ignore

        repeated incidents of feeblemindedness

You have an irrational irritation.
as if they could call their old self back
    be who they were
if only they wanted to enough.

When you're vulnerable
you should be protected
by those who love you.

                "All my life we've had pitted prunes,
                Now when I need them we don't."

He's so dear
I check him out at our little town's
Chamber of Commerce social.
seated, he looks so small now
this bent over little man
smiling with admiration and warmth
at all the people and bustle around him.
My father who once stood so tall
and strong in every sense.

He thought for himself
defiant of corrupt influence no matter wealth or power
Pride
never afraid to stand alone
Principled
when the carpenter's union offered him a position
he said look at all the Negro carpenters we have now
its time that they had a representative.

It is not possible to love someone more
                and not burst

                How do we measure things?

                Maybe like a wise parent
                forcing self-restraint
                to allow trial and error
                - the natural course.
                I should have pulled back.
                But I couldn't stand to see
                that beloved form hurt,
                any fall or bump
                – those horrid maroon bruises
                exaggerated by the blood thinner.
                once the way his paper skin
                rubbed off his forearm

We all must die
We all must pass through that membrane

        He'd start conversations with anyone he'd meet
        doctor's waiting rooms
        to your initial embarrassment
        though the serious-faced stranger
        would always transmute – smiling, happy to reply.
        With Dad's hearing these were more
        smiling overtures of friendliness
                than real exchanges.
            I could observe myself
            as this pushing impatient presence
            - let's get this appointment over with -
            forsaking the most important things in life
                savoring the moment
                whatever was given
                and people.

After his 90th birthday celebration
we saved all the cards in a basket by his chair.
Every time he'd fish them out and go through them
it was a first encounter.
Gladdened by the warm sentiments from cherished friends
yet this was bizarre

you knew his memory couldn't hold it
beyond that moment
so of what value was the exercise?

                        May 25th, in bed
                        in the morning,
                            "I'm too old for this."
                        He's not sleepy-dopey,
                            or kidding,
                        it's a sane sober assessment.

He loved to be driven around the valley
arriving back home he'd always say,
   "Thanks for the buggy ride."

                      Because I do believe in the eternal
                      I wondered how his real (whole) self
                      would view his weakened behavior
                          and our treatment of him.

O Dad I would have liked your last years
to have been different.
but look, even with you half lost
I couldn't let go.

                        June 23rd just lying in bed
                        he asks,
                           "What do I have to do
                              to be safe?"
                        a question - not to me -
                           a wondering out loud.
                        There's nothing I can say.

                You can take all your great men of history
                famous for power and accomplishments
                      those in Politics
                        in Science
                      or in the Arts

                    the brilliant
                    the daring
          I wouldn't trade any or all of them
          for my humble father.

declared dead.
so worn out from not sleeping, out of my mind,
I'm cleaning his body
before the guys from the Neptune Society arrive,
I speak to his body
   "You know I loved you Dad.
     All my life I loved you."

                Though I don't believe in death
                don't believe the body is the person,
                and with all the years I had to prepare,
                the fact that I could go on living
                and you would not be in my world now
                    is still such a blow

My love for you will never fade
Beyond the beauty of the lapsing sunset,
the Ocean's grandeur – that scale beyond,
the motionless timeless lakes
    set in the mountains,
the passionate consuming human dramas,
    the thick diverse life of Nature's plants;
When all these wonders wrapt in the Earth
    with its own great age,
exist only as memory of a past
My love for you will hold undiminished

The death of our closest readies us
     as nothing else does
as we stand on the shore
to face our own crossing

I will not be separated from my father.
    My fate joined to his
        forever

Sometimes good is good
light is light

www.ingramcontent.com/pod-product-compliance
Lightning Source LLC
Chambersburg PA
CBHW022054160426
43198CB00008B/229